Anglican Churches of
Derbyshire

I.A.H. Combes

To Christopher
with thanks for his tireless
help and support.

Anglican Churches of
Derbyshire

I.A.H. Combes

Landmark Publishing

Published by

Ashbourne Hall, Cokayne Ave
Ashbourne, Derbyshire DE6 1EJ England
Tel: (01335) 347349 Fax: (01335) 347303
e-mail: landmark@clara.net
web site: www.landmarkpublishing.co.uk

1st edition

ISBN: 1-84306-152-X

British Library Cataloguing in Publication Data: a catalogue
record for this book is available from the British Library.

Printed by CPI Bath.

Design & reproduction by James Allsopp, Mark Titerton & Simon Hartshorne

Front cover: St Mary and All Saints, Chesterfield.

Back cover:

Top left: The Foljanbe memorial, All Saints, Bakewell. *Top middle*: The apse, All Saints, Steetley. *Top right*: Wrought iron screen, Derby Cathedral. *Bottom*: St Giles, Matlock.

Page 3: St John the Evangelist, Derby.

Photography by the author unless stated.
The line Black & White drawings are by Godfrey Meynell unless stated.

Contents

Contents

Contents

Introduction

Of all the landmarks in Derbyshire, little seems more permanent than the churches that punctuate our landscape, villages and towns. Houses and farms may come and go but the local church is ever there, unchanging from time immemorial. In this age of increasing change and restlessness, the churches are ever more the only consistent reminders of another, more stable past. Or so it would seem. In fact, go back only a couple of hundred years or so, and the churches around us were very different places indeed. Rather than unshakeable monuments of ancient faith, the church buildings of Derbyshire are survivors and reflections of the changes and upheavals of the centuries which have passed since the Christianisation of the country and continue to be so as they face the changes of the future.

Although the Christianisation of England is mainly credited to Augustine of Canterbury, the kingdom of Mercia, with its capital at Repton, was largely converted by the efforts of Diuma and three other priests who came here from Lindisfarne to convert the kingdom to Christianity. Diuma was eventually buried at Repton in 658. Of the Saxon churches of Derbyshire, only traces remain, such as the extraordinary life of Christ preserved at Wirksworth and the innumerable Saxon crosses set in the

Saxon coffin lid, dating from c800.

churchyards. Of the buildings themselves, but little has survived; largely because the majority of Saxon churches in this area were constructed of wood, but also because of the great upheaval which changed the face of the country forever – the Norman Conquest. The country's new overlords rapidly took control of the churches, suppressing and discouraging the traditional Anglo-Saxon dedications to such native saints as St Wystan and St Werburgh and introducing their own architectural styles, most significantly the almost exclusive use of stone in the building of churches, of which there was now an explosion in numbers as a result of one of the most enthusiastic periods of church building in the country's history, the like of which would not be seen again until the 19th century. The traces of this time can be seen in the Norman remnants which still survive in many rural churches and the few complete Norman churches still in existence, such as that of Melbourne. It is an architectural style characterised by round arches, thick walls and small windows, all embellished with distinctive zigzag patterns and sometimes animal and human forms. Cruciform layouts were particularly popular for the most significant churches.

The Domesday Survey of 1086 gives the first almost complete picture of the existence of the churches in the country. It makes careful record of the churches and priests attached to the manors. At this time, William the Conqueror dispossessed the native aristocracy and, seizing the manors of the county, handed them out to his own courtiers. Of these, the most significant for Derbyshire were his illegitimate son William Peverel and the Norman nobleman Henry de Ferrers, who along with Walter D'Eincourt and Ralph Fitzhurbert, now came into the possession of literally hundreds of royal manors with their estates and churches. This period saw also the widespread founding of abbeys and priories at places such as Tutbury. Very many of the churches that came into the hands of the Norman nobility were promptly handed over to these institutions, partly so that these should take responsibility for providing clergy for the churches, but mostly so that the abbeys and priories could benefit from the lucrative tithes and glebe incomes.

There were far fewer parish churches at this time than one might expect. Many of the old village churches we see today were not, in the first place, churches in their own right at all. Rather, they were chapels of ease, belonging to a larger mother church and built for the convenience of the local inhabitants who lived at too great a distance from the mother church to be able to attend it regularly. Those who attended these chapels would still be expected to have obligations to the mother church and to worship there upon major festivals. The mother church would also have held the rights to burials and baptisms, and the fees arising from those. Hence, for example, the churches of Kniveton, Mapleton, Thorpe, Fenny Bentley, Bradley and Edlaston were all originally simply chapels of St Oswald's church in Ashbourne. The vicar at Ashbourne had the duty to provide clergy for these chapels and they in turn had reciprocal duties to the mother church. Very many of these mother churches were moreover, in the possession and under the supervision of the priories and abbeys. One of the great beneficiaries of this was the Chapter and Dean of Lincoln who came into the possession of many of the parishes of the area and were notorious for their grasping of the incomes of the churches as illustrated in the rood screen of Fenny Bentley. St Oswald's church was held by the Dean and Chapter of Lincoln – the Dean of Lincoln being Rector of Ashbourne.

In this way, the abbeys and cathedrals came to hold sway over vast wealth while, in many cases, failing to honour their own obligations to the parishes in their care. This situation contributed towards the resentment felt against them by much of the populace, their downfall during the Reformation, and the subsequent dissolution of the monasteries in 1536-40. Suddenly the power of the priories and abbeys vanished, their property seized by the Crown and passing rapidly from thence into private hands. Along with this property, came the churches with their income and advowsons (the right to appoint clergy). Church building in England virtually ceased for the next 100 years as churches were instead adapted and reordered to suit the growing protestant spirit of the age. Focus moved away from the altar to the pulpit, and box pews, for which rents could be charged, were installed – all things beginning to shift towards making the church comfortable so that long sermons and readings might be better endured and digested. As the anti-Catholic fury gained momentum, ancient fonts, crosses and statues were cast out, the altar at the east end replaced with a communion table in the nave, and the Book of Common Prayer replaced with the Directory of Public Worship. Churches were now, more than ever, put to use as secular as well as religious buildings: they housed schools and were even at times put to use as prisons.

The precedent had been set that the church properties could be claimed by the state and this went a step further in 1649 when the Commonwealth government, desperate for cash to pay the enormous army, abolished Deans and Chapters on 30th April 1649 and appointed the Parliamentary Commissioners in 1650 to carry out a survey of their properties to see what could be sold. These Commissioners recommended the widespread closing of churches and their amalgamation with nearby parishes. It appears, though, that frequently its recommendations were ignored and many of the churches continued. Indeed, from 1704, a large number of these small chapelries were enabled to become parish churches in their own right, thanks to a fund known as Queen Anne's Bounty which gave grants intended to augment the chapel's funds so that its clergy could be paid a living stipend. Such grants could be made outright or as matching grants where others had agreed to make an initial benefaction. The Bounty, however, was only partially successful in its aims and poverty remained a severe problem among the clergy of smaller and/or less affluent parishes.

By the beginning of the 19th century, many churches were in a desperate state. The troubles of the previous centuries, the destruction brought about by the Reformation and Civil War and the growing problems of social disaffection here and abroad had all left their scars and the ancient churches were showing their age. Many were in a ruinous and barely usable condition, their windows and roofs decayed, fonts removed and wall paintings obliterated with plaster and whitewash. The small, crumbling churches, many of which had survived since Norman, even Saxon times, now seemed inadequate to the needs of the early 19th century religious revival and the growing populations in cities, manufacturing towns and around the mills and factories. The Act for Promoting the Building of Additional Churches in Populous Parishes was passed in 1818 and the Incorporated Church Building Society came into being. Funds from the state were now made available for the building of new churches, under the supervision of the Commissioners for Building New Churches (1815), leading to the building of 214 large churches, now known as Commissioners' or Waterloo (from the battle which had taken place at this time) churches. A taste for heavy square Greek revival buildings predominated at first, especially among the London churches, sometimes moderated with a few pointed Gothic elements, but such buildings were expensive, with their columns and stone porticos, so the Commissioners soon began to favour a less imposing Pointed Gothic revival. Funds were also given by the Incorporated Church Building Society to expand present churches, with

St John the Evangelist, Buxton. The church was built with a heavy portico at the east, but this was later filled in to form a chancel.

the intention of providing more seating in churches which, full of rented box pews, often had no seating space for those of more limited means, even when most of the pews were empty.

Briefs submitted for the repair and restoration of churches catalogue neglect which had allowed the buildings to degenerate so much as to be not only uncomfortable but downright dangerous. Archdeacon Butler in 1823 complained of St Werburgh in Blackwell that:

"The church has been suffered to go into a state of most ruinous decay. It is unsafe, nay highly dangerous for the parishioners to assemble in it in windy weather, and any attempt at temporary repairs will only subject them to further expense as it is impossible to do it effectively. The parishioners are highly to blame and have nothing but their own neglect to thank."

That particular church was pulled down at the Archdeacon's insistence and was replaced with a new structure, much against the will of the churchwardens who would have preferred to repair and preserve the original building. This was no isolated example – few churches escaped extensive restoration at this time, and there were plenty that were replaced altogether.

While many of the Commissioners' churches of the early period amounted to little more than 'preaching boxes' with a few nods to the Pointed Gothic, this was rapidly overtaken by the Oxford and Cambridge movements which brought about the Victorian Gothic revival in 1855-1885. With such architects as A.W. Pugin (1812-52), Street and Butterfield as its foremost proponents, this movement sought to take the church back to its older and medieval traditions and to rediscover the sense of sanctity and mystery which, they argued, had been lost during the Reformation. The Cambridge Camden Society, which became the Ecclesiological Society in 1845, held up the Decorated Period (1290 –1350) as the proper model for church building. In this wave of enthusiasm, many churches disappeared, with large, gothic buildings rising in their place.

We are fortunate for the contribution of such local historians as Godfrey Meynell in 1817 who, part of the new and growing antiquarian movement, went about the churches of Derbyshire, cataloguing their features of interest and making sketches which are now the only evidence that remains of many of the ancient chapels which were thrown down at this time and replaced with new, ambitious Victorian structures. The lucky churches were well restored – especially well done are those that came under the supervision of Sir George Gilbert Scott who restored such treasures as St Oswald's in Ashbourne and All Saints in Bakewell. Others were replaced altogether with new buildings of varying merit, the best being those of H.I. Stevens.

At the beginning of the 20th century, these ideals were blossoming into the Arts and Crafts movement, which combined the theological ideals with Pugin with a horror of the 'dark satanic mills' and their cheap, industrial productions. Now the gothic revival was to be a longing for the skill of the craftsman and village, for a medieval world of integrity and beauty where everything made should reflect the highest standards of integrity and craftsmanship. William Morris founded Morris, Marshall, Faulkner & Co, later simply Morris & Co, producing wallpaper and tapestries but more importantly for churches, the medieval stained glass to be found in so many Derbyshire churches, for the most part designed by Burne-Jones for the company. In architecture, one of the most important practitioners in Derbyshire was P.H. Currey, notable for his sensitive restorations and for churches such as St Mary's in Buxton and St Osmund's, Wilmorton. The most dramatic example of this movement is the church in Langley Mill, but the influence was felt almost everywhere.

It was a great time for church architecture, but it was not to last. The first World War was soon upon them, and there was no heart or money left for ambitious building. A number of churches started around this time were never finished to their original plan, and left truncated and awkward by lack of funds. In 1927, the Derby diocese was created, separating Derbyshire from the Southwell diocese and it was clear to the new bishop that more buildings were needed to keep up with the changing and expanding population. The next 70 years saw much achieved in the rebuilding of derelict churches and the erection of new buildings, though few showed the scale and ambition of previous centuries.

Church architecture has never entirely recovered since. Wealthy patrons and even rectors able single-handedly to finance restorations or rebuilding were gone and a growing preoccupation with heritage and conservation started to arrest the organic growth of churches which had been in a constant process of change and evolution since the earliest days. Churches are often perceived as much older than they are and entirely immutable. The arguments on both sides are powerful – ill considered changes in the past have destroyed or vandalised churches which would be treasures today, yet it would be a pity if all that the present generations could contribute would be the addition of kitchens and lavatories, useful as these might be. In some places, tiny or unusable churches have been brought back to life with bold and imaginative rebuilding, Holymoorside for example, with its pretty, airy interior and in others, new churches have been attractively integrated with social centres, as at the church on Oakwood. Others however, have become museums to their own past, with endless display boards and warnings against photography or touching the monuments. While there is no doubt that mistakes have been made and some buildings have suffered dreadful vandalism through ill-conceived alterations, it is also the case that, clever and useful adaptations have added to the usefulness of many churches and kept on the onward flow of development which makes a church a living continuation of the past rather than a monument to a nearly forgotten time. Let us hope that in coming centuries our own time will have left something behind able to inspire the next.

Sources

For the early history of the churches, I am much indebted to J.C. Cox, whose great 1875 survey of the history and condition of the churches of Derbyshire has never been equalled. Most useful has been his dedication in studying the ancient ecclesiastical documents – he has extracted fascinating passages from church registers, correspondence and notes as well as from the great collection of Briefs held at the British Library and Lambeth. I have unashamedly borrowed these, providing as they do such a vivid insight into the human past of the churches. It is from his researches that I have also taken all the extracts from the reports of the Parliamentary Commissioners in 1650. In his personal visits to the churches, Cox also recorded fascinating anecdotes and peculiarities which were already rapidly fading away as the modern world advanced upon them. He shows us a world where ancient Norman fonts had only just been rescued from use as chopping boards for butchers and washbasins for schoolboys; he found churches still being used as school houses during the week and laments irreplaceable antiquities destroyed in the haste for rebuilding and modernisation.

Another important and dedicated antiquarian of the period was Llewellyn Fredrick William Jewitt who founded *The Reliquary* which was first published in July 1860 and represents one of the very first serious antiquarian periodicals and which, although it very much focused on Derbyshire, also enjoyed a wider circulation. Such periodicals were the forerunners of the modern archaeology by which they were succeeded. Jewitt continued to edit *The Reliquary* until 1886, contributing a large number of articles and observations of his own. In 1886, he was succeeded by J.C. Cox who continued in that role until 1909, by which time it had become *The Reliquary and Illustrated Archaeologist*. Its articles ranged widely, especially in the early days from studies and sketches of architectural styles to records of local ballads and legends. It is an invaluable resource. Lyson's *Derbyshire* is equally interesting and a good source for local customs such as rush bearing and maiden's garlands.

No study of buildings in England would be complete without reference to Pevsner's magisterial summary of the country's important buildings and I have made much use of his volume on Derbyshire – the only disadvantage of his work being that it is, if anything, too well known and his words on local churches will be already more than familiar to the great army of dedicated local historians whose work can be seen as leaflets and booklets in so many local churches. The standard of these is frequently high and I am grateful for their presence. There are too many of these to mention individually, but where a church has one I have almost certainly purchased and consulted it. It is only to be regretted, however, that these are usually only to be found in earlier churches. All churches have at one time been modern buildings and we should not devalue or lose the history of those which at present only have a few decades to boast of. It would be good to see the more recent churches having the confidence to write about their own histories in greater detail, especially as the Church has in general lost the tradition of using the Church registers as a diary of day to day events. These modern churches, therefore, have been more of a challenge for research than our more well documented architectural gems and it is a sign of the changing nature of research that I soon found myself with a list of websites to add to the bibliography – these have been a valuable source of information on more recent buildings which have not yet made their way into books and histories.

Lastly I was fortunate enough to be given access to the Revd J.O. Drackley's booklet 'Notes on the Churches of Derbyshire' which was designed to serve as a resource to the Derby Diocese Advisory Committee and which corrects some of the errors to be found in Pevsner. I have, in most cases where there is disagreement, followed his dating.

Acknowledgements

My thanks first of all to the many clergymen/women and church wardens who opened their churches for me and often contributed information and anecdotes which I could not have found elsewhere.

I would also like to thank Godfrey Meynell who gave me access to the Meynell manuscripts – the fascinating collection of sketches and information compiled by his ancestor Godfrey Meynell in 1813.

Anthony Short and Mark Parsons generously gave time to read the manuscript and add their comments. Thanks also to Dr Lynn Willies for information concerning the lead smelting mill in Cromford.

This project grew out of my work for the Derby Diocesan Advisory Committee for whom I have been compiling a database of the Derbyshire Churches. My thanks to them for their support and the initial inspiration. The photographs are all by the author and those of the interior of Derby Cathedral appear by kind permission of the Dean and Chapter.

Note:
It would be beyond the scope of a work such as this to provide an exhaustive history of every church included. I have limited myself therefore to a few points of interest – which I hope will inspire further reading and research on the part of those so inclined. For the sake of consistency, moreover, I have chosen to include only parish churches in the Diocese of Derby, which meant omitting Taxal but including such churches as Steetley Chapel (which is part of the Diocese but not of the county). Although I have generally omitted all those churches which are, or are in the process of being made redundant, I have made an exception for Ballidon Chapel because of its charm and interest. There are a few churches – generally small and modern – concerning whose history I have managed to glean almost nothing, and I would be delighted to hear from anyone who wishes to share any information about them.

On architectural styles:
For each church I have indicated, where possible, the general architectural style that it most closely represents (in some cases the century to which its style most closely belongs). This is meant only as a rough guide to the reader, who should be aware that in some cases so many different styles are present that the church cannot be given any specific designation. For 19th and 20th century churches I have indicated, where appropriate, that style of architecture which is, to a greater or lesser extent, being emulated.

Aldercar, St John

19th century: Decorated style
This was built as a chapel of ease by Stevens & Robinson for the parish of Langley Mill, in 1871. The east window is by W. Ramsey. The church was enlarged in 1928-29 by Naylor & Sale.

Alderwasley, All Saints

19th century: Early English style
A private chapel may have been built here by the Fawne family, perhaps in the 14th century, though more solid evidence for it can be found during the reign of Henry VIII, in the indenture for the repair and dedication of a chapel "in the honor of Seynt Margaret". The Parliamentary Commissioners in 1650 mention the chapel and state that it "may conveniently be disused". A new church was built in 1850 for F. E. Hurt of Alderwasley Hall. This served as a private chapel until 1931 when it became a chapel of ease in the Wirksworth parish, replacing the 15th century church of St Margaret, now the village hall. It was reroofed in the 1970s by A. Short & Partners.

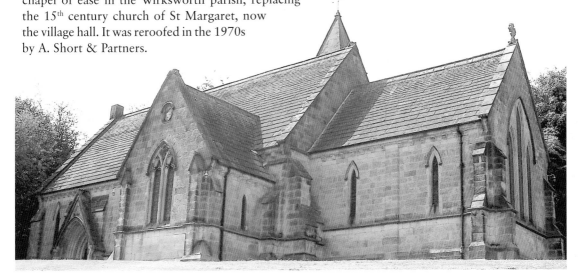

Alfreton, St Martin

14th century and Perpendicular
The church dates back to c.1170 and was probably founded by Robert FizRanulph (or FizRalph). Nave, south aisle and tower are mostly 14th and 15th century, though the ground floor and lower parts of the tower are 13th century. The north aisle was rebuilt and the church generally enlarged in 1868 by T.C. Hine and the chancel was lengthened

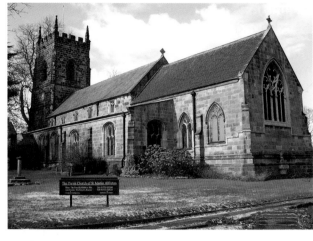

in 1899-1901. The chancel screen dates from 1921 and now bears figures from the church of St Andrew in Derby which was demolished in 1968. The church was recently repaired by A. Short & Partners following a fire and during these repairs, part of the west floor was lowered to provide for a children's area.

Alkmonton, St John

19th century: Early English style
In 1406, a hospital for female lepers was refounded here, the previous one having fallen into disuse. This Hospital of St Leonard also acquired around this time a chapel where prayers were to be said for the founder and her family. By this time, the hospital sheltered not female lepers but seven poor men and a master in charge of them. Some time after 1474, a bequest of Walter Blount, Lord Montjoy led to the building of a chapel dedicated to St Nicholas, intended, according to the Chantry Roll of Henry VIII, to serve "for a pste to saye masse and to praye for his soule his ancestors sowls and all crystyan sowlls".

There is no trace left of either the hospital or the chapel, but the present church which was built in 1843, contains the chapel's font.

This is the only church in Derbyshire to have been built with flint walls.

Allenton & Shelton Lock, St Edmund

20th century: Gothic
This church was built in 1939 by Eaton of Derby using white Mansfield stone.

Allestree, St Edmund

19th century
This was originally a chapel of Mackworth and remained so until the 19th century. Oddly, and inaccurately, the Parliamentary Commissioners said the following: "Allestree is a viccaridge and parsonage impropriate worth about three score pounds per annum the same Mr Francis Mundye is Impropriator receives the profits and procures the place supplied. Mr Botham is curate insufficient and a drunkard. Allestree is a small parish and may conveniently be united to Aukmonds in Derby it lying neare."

The church was rebuilt and enlarged in 1865-7 by Stevens & Robinson of Derby, incorporating a Norman south doorway, the east wall of the chancel and the 13th century west tower.

William Evans (who also financed the building of St Peter's church in Parwich) paid for the restoration of this church and for the tower clock which was added in 1856.

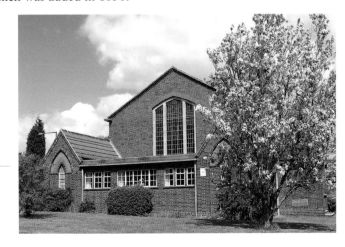

Allestree, St Nicholas

20th century: Simplified gothic
Built in 1957-8 by Peter Woore.

Alsop-en-le-Dale, St Michael and All Angels

Norman and neo-Norman

The Alsop-en-le-Dale chapel, one of the chapelries of Ashbourne, was founded in the 12th century and still retains its Norman nave and doorway, as well as a font of the same period. The tower, however, is imitation Norman and was added in 1882-3 by F.J. Robinson. The Parliamentary Commissioners in 1650 recommended that the chapel be disused and united to Parwich, but the chapel later became a parish church for Alsop-en-le-Dale.

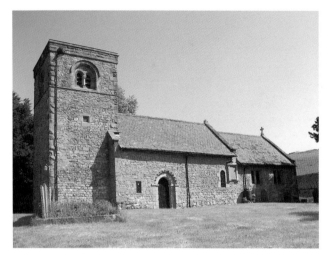

The Millennium window by Henry Haig.

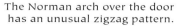
The Norman arch over the door has an unusual zigzag pattern.

Alvaston, St Michael, and All Angels

19th century: Decorated style

There was already a church and priest here by the time of the Domesday Survey and this was given to Darley Abbey by William Fitzralph. It appears to have become a vicarage soon after as there was a vicar here by 1170. Of it the Parliamentary Commissioners reported: "Michaells is a viccaridge really worth eight pounds per annum (...) Michaells is fitt to be disused and united to the parish of All Saints (Derby)". The church was used by the congregation of All Saints during the rebuilding of that church in 1723-5.

The *Derby Mercury* records that on 17th August 1856, "Between five and ten minutes to 12 o'clock . . . shortly before the conclusion of the sermon, the gable end of St Michael's church, Derby, gave way, and

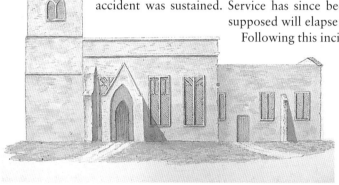

the casing fell with a heavy crash into the churchyard. The fall of the material shook the fabric of the church and, as might be expected spread consternation through those assembled within its walls. The service was prematurely concluded and the congregation, in a state of great terror and alarm, hurried out of the sacred edifice. Fortunately no accident was sustained. Service has since been suspended and some little time it is supposed will elapse before it is resumed."

Following this incident, a new building by H.I. Stevens was erected in 1855-6, and rededicated in 1858. A brass plaque in the church commemorates this rebuilding : "To the glory of God and for the souls of men this Church was rebuilt on the site of the ancient parish church of unknown antiquity, the chancel of which fell during divine service on Aug 17th 1856."

Ambergate, St Anne

19th century: Early English style

This church by A. Coke Hill was opened and dedicated in 1892 but not consecrated until 1897.

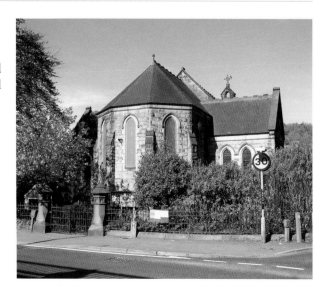

Ashbourne, St Oswald

Mainly Early English and Decorated

The Domesday Survey records that Ashbourne had a church and a priest. It was given, along with its chapelries and the church at Chesterfield, to Lincoln Cathedral by William Rufus in 1093. There was thus undoubtedly a Saxon church here, though nothing of this remains. Excavations in 1913 showed a Norman crypt but the oldest surviving part of the church still extant is the chancel. This must date from around 1241, when the church was dedicated to St Oswald as attested by the brass plaque, now in the Lady Chapel. Said to have been originally intended as a minster, this is certainly one of the outstanding churches of Derbyshire. The spire is 212ft high, with length of the nave and chancel at 176ft.

The clerestory was added in c1520. The church was extensively repaired at the beginning of the 18th century and alterations were made in 1839-40 though a more important restoration was carried out around 1876 under the direction of George Gilbert Scott.

J. C. Cox

The wrought iron churchyard gates are c.1730 by Bakewell and were restored by Chris Topp of York in the late 1990s.

The east window is by Kempe with fragments of medieval glass.

The 1905 Turnbull window, in memory of sisters Monica and Dorothy, who were killed in a fire. It is by Christopher Whall and is one of the finest examples of 20th century Pre-Raphaelite stained glass in the country.

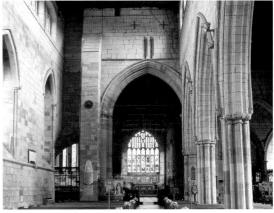

The unusual and very asymmetrical nave.

The ancient brass plaque marking the dedication of the church. Translation: In the 1241st year from the incarnation of our Lord, on the 8th day after the kalends of May, this church and this altar were consecrated in honour of the saint Oswald, king and martyr, by the venerable father in the Lord, Hugo de Patishul, the bishop of Coventry. This brass plaque is the second oldest of its kind in Europe.

The north chapel contains an notable collection of tombs from the Cokayne family as well as Thomas Banke's famous 1793 Boothby tomb for the five-year-old Penelope Boothby.

Ashbourne, St John

Adapted Romanesque

The church was built in 1871 to accommodate a congregation which had split off from that at St Oswald's church. It has interior pillars of cast iron. It was built by Francis Wright of Osmaston Manor, who was a director of the Butterley Company ironworks and who provided the ironwork for St Pancras Station in London.

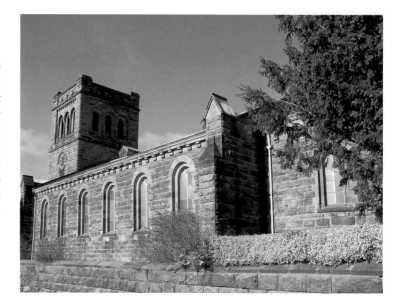

Ashford in the Water, Holy Trinity

Various

There has been a chapel on this site since the 12th century, but the present church mostly dates from the 1868-70 rebuilding by J. M. and H. Taylor. The exception is the tower which is largely 14th century but whose lower levels may be quite early. There is a Norman tympanum showing the tree of life flanked by a lion and a pig (J. Cox calls it "a wild boar and a wolf"). The arcade is 14th century.

The church also contains stained glass depicting the Annunciation by William Morris and St John & St Gregory by Burne-Jones.

An interesting insight into church life at this time appears in a 1632 document cited by Cox, which concerns seating in the church and is entitled: "A Perfect order how men are to Sitt in the Chapell of Ashford by the Official Mr Rowlandson and the neighbours of Ashford Aprill the 10th, 1632". This stipulated that men should sit on the south side of the church and the women on the north, while the seat "under the Pulpitt is for the Minister's wife whom soever she is".

Ashover, All Saints

Perpendicular

The Domesday book records a church and priest for Ashover, but the present building dates from between 1350 and 1419. There are, however, earlier elements such as the 1275 porch with the crowned heads of Edward I and Queen Eleanor which was built as a thanksgiving when the estates, confiscated by Henry IV, were returned by Edward I. The head at the apex is held to be that of Margery Reresby who had the arch built. The tower is supposed to be 1419 and completed by the Babington family, while the stone coffin at its base dates from 1200.

The Babingtons also gave the rood screen in the early 16th century.

The traces of the original roof can be seen in the stonework. In the 16th century the roof was raised and a clerestory added. The belfry contains a bell with Napoleon's name, due to the fact that it had cracked while ringing the news of Napoleon's abdication in 1814 and had to be recast.

The church was restored in 1843.

This alabaster tomb of Thomas Babington (1518) and his wife Editha, is an outstanding example of its kind. Cox, in 1875, says that the effigies are both painted, with the exception of the hands and faces, "in dull colours – red and green predominating". These would not have been the original colours. The tomb was actually built by Thomas Babington for his wife who predeceased him. He is buried alongside, as he did not want the tomb to be broken into for his sake.

Below: 'Weepers' around the sides of the Babington tomb.

The church possesses one of the only 30 Norman lead fonts in the country. It is dated 1150 and was saved from being melted down for bullets during the Civil War (the fate of most of the lead fonts), by Immanuel Bourne who buried it in his kitchen garden.

Aston on Trent, All Saints

Various

Two churches are associated with this area by the Domesday Survey and these would probably have been Aston on Trent and Weston on Trent. The advowson of the church was in earlier times held by the Abbey of St Werburgh at Chester, but after the dissolution of the monasteries, this passed to the Bishop of Chester and later into private hands.

Some parts of the church may be late Saxon. There is a Norman west tower and door along with some Norman windows and tower arch. The nave is 13th century as is the font. The church was restored in 1849.

Atlow, S.S. Philip and James

19th century: Early English style

Atlow was one of the chapels of Bradbourne at the time when the latter and its chapels were made over to the Priory of Dunstable. The chapel itself is first mentioned in the Chronicles of Dunstable in 1278. The Parliamentary Survey in 1650 said of Atlow that "Mr Massey is a curate and has ffoure shillings a week salarye, a man unfit and a drunkard" and went on to point out that "Attlowe lyes remote from Bradbourne, and maye conveniently

be united to Hognastone."

The chapel was rebuilt in the mid 19th century, leaving only traces of the original structure, and then again in 1874 by Stevens & Robinson (designed by H.I. Stevens before his death in 1873) in the Early English style. At this time the dedication was changed from All Saints to Saints Philip and James. No traces of the original chapel now survive.

Ault Hucknall, St John the Baptist

Saxon and Norman

The west front, north arcade and east arch of the crossing (an ambitious one for such a small church) are Saxon or very early Norman although no mention of this church is made in the Domesday Survey. The "Savage Window" at the east end of the south aisle dates from 1527and beneath this, at the foot of the 1627 monument to Anne Keighley (wife of the first Earl of Devonshire) is a slab to the philosopher Thomas Hobbes who died at Hardwick in 1679.

The church was much altered during the Perpendicular period and restored in 1885-8 by Butterfield who also added the tiled floor.

Details from the chancel arch.

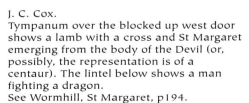

J. C. Cox.
Tympanum over the blocked up west door shows a lamb with a cross and St Margaret emerging from the body of the Devil (or, possibly, the representation is of a centaur). The lintel below shows a man fighting a dragon.
See Wormhill, St Margaret, p194.

Bakewell, All Saints

Mainly 12th and 13th century with later additions

The town of Bakewell is first mentioned in the historical records in 924, when, according to the *Anglo-Saxon Chronicle*, King Edward came to Bakewell and gave orders that a castle should be built and garrisoned nearby.

In the Domesday Survey, Bakewell is recorded as having a church and two priests. There would thus have been a church here well before 1066, but of this little more than fragments remain as the building was replaced in 1110, probably by William Peverel. The new building was of a large, cruciform plan and underwent alterations in 1250 and again around 1300, the octagonal tower and spire being added at the end of the 14th, beginning of the 15th century. The west front is Norman with a Norman doorway and blocked Norman arches, but the remainder of the church underwent rebuilding and restoration in the 19th century. The tower and spire were deemed to be in danger of collapse in 1825 and the spire was demolished at that time, the tower following it in 1830. The church underwent repair and rebuilding in 1841 – 1852 by William Flockton, at which time the tower and spire were rebuilt as were the transepts and the Vernon chapel. New pews were put in and the Norman arches in the nave were replaced with Gothic arches.

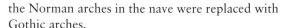

The churchyard contains a number of interesting epitaphs, including one to Thomas Stafford who "while working at the north arch of the tower of Bakewell church was by an accident suddenly cut off in the prime of life and vigour of health . . ." and the following, supposedly by Charles Wesley, in memory of Esther Leedham, who died aged 3 years and 3 months:

> *Beneath a sleeping infant lies*
> *To earth whose body lent*
> *More glorious shall hereafter rise*
> *Tho' not more innocent.*
> *When the Archangel's trump shall blow*
> *And souls to bodies join*
> *Thousands shall wish their life below*
> *Had been as short as thine.*

Sadly, the gravestone is now so badly damaged as to be entirely illegible, apart from the last two lines – the text is only preserved in such records as Black's *Directory of Derby*.

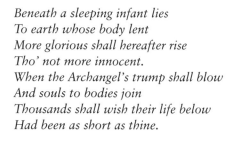

The chancel was restored in 1879–82 under the direction of G.G. Scott the younger (with Temple Moor), who added the reredos and altar by Ninian Comper, the mosaic floor, choir stalls and the screen depicting the 'Seven Acts of Mercy'. The east window is 1892 by Burlison & Grylls.

The restorations of the 19th century uncovered huge numbers of Norman and Saxon, including 57 coffin lids, some of which are on display in the church and, as above, in the porch.

The Foljambe memorial, 1385.

The font probably dates from the 14th century.

Ballidon, All Saints

Early Norman (much restored)
Ballidon was one of the chapelries of
Bradbourne which later passed into the
hands of the Priory of Dunstable. The south
doorway is said to be Norman, renewed in
the 19th century (though the door does not
appear in Meynell's sketch, indicating that
it may be a 19th century copy) and the
chancel arch is similarly renewed. The east
window is late 15th century. There is a
fireplace high on the west wall, which would
have heated a small room probably for the
use of the priest from Bradbourne on his
visits.

Until 1822, there were, apparently, pen and ink frescoes
on the walls, but these met with the disapproval of the
churchwardens, who decided that they made the chapel look
a 'bad place' and had them plastered over. At this time plaster
ceilings were added and pews put in for the first time.

The Parliamentary Commissioners of 1650 say that
Ballidon "is a chappell apperteyning (to Bradbourn), Mr
Thomas Miles is viccar, a man of good repute. Mr W. Alsop
serves the chappell at Ballington, a man unfit for the ministry
and scandalous." The church is now in the process of being
made redundant – it is much to be hoped that some way
will be found of keeping this unique little chapel open.

One of the chapel's most interesting features is this well
preserved (probably 15th century but possibly Norman)
but somewhat bizarre font – the figures on its top band
are upside down, those in the middle have no top or
bottom and those on the third band are the right way up.

Bamford, St John the Baptist

19th century: Early English style
This church with its tall, narrow spire, unusual for Derbyshire, is by Butterfield, who also designed the vicarage. The church was consecrated on 17th October 1860. The stained glass is all by Frederick Preedy of Evesham.

Barlborough, St James

Mainly 19th century: Perpendicular style
The church and priest of Barlborough are possibly mentioned in the Domesday Book, though the reference may be to the one at Whitwell. The oldest part of the church, which was originally dedicated to St Margaret, dates to c. 1200, or possibly earlier. It was probably rebuilt in the 16th century and was again rebuilt and restored in the 18th century. The north aisle, south arcade and clerestory were added in 1894-9 by G.B. Bulmer.

(Great) Barlow, St Laurence

Norman and NeoNorman

The original church consisted of a Norman nave and short chancel. There was a plan to demolish the building in 1784 and permission for this was granted on account of it being in such bad condition that it was "in daily danger of falling down, so that the inhabitants cannot attend but at hazard of their lives" (1784 Brief, recorded in Cox). However, it seems that the needed amount of £1020 4s 1d failed to materialise, and so the building was spared. A neo-Norman chancel was added by S. Rollinson in 1867. The original chancel contains a 13th century window, and the west window is 17th century. It appears that there was originally a larger steeple in the place of the present small bell tower.

Barrow Hill, St Andrew

19th century: Early English style
Built in 1893-5 by Parker & Unwin to provide a building for the church, which originally shared the 1856 school building nearby. It was consecrated on 29th April 1895.

Barrow on Trent, St Wilifrid

Various

Barrow on Trent is recorded in the Domesday Survey as having a priest and a church. This church was given by Robert de Bakepuze to the Priory of St John of Jerusalem (Knights Hospitallers) during the reign of Henry II, and remained in their hands, having been annexed to Yeaveley, until the order was dissolved by Henry III.

After the dissolution, the church passed into private hands. The Parliamentary Commissioners in 1650 recommended that it be united to Swarkstone.

No remains of the Norman church survive. The north nave arcade is 13th century and is the oldest part of the church. Other parts are 14th and 15th with some 19th century alterations. There is a 14th century alabaster effigy of a priest. The church had a collection of heraldic glass which appears to have been destroyed during the 1818 restoration.

Baslow, St Anne

Many Decorated
Over 800 years old, the church was originally a chapelry of Bakewell at the time of King John's reign. Nothing remains of the original Norman fabric and the oldest part is the tower and spire, probably dating from the second half of the 13th century. The building was restored in 1852-53. The chancel was rebuilt in 1911. Part of a Saxon cross may be found in the porch and the latter has built into it an ancient coffin stone, which is probably about 700 years old.

Beeley, St Anne

Various
The church is Norman in origin and dates from c1150. The Norman south door survives, as does the 13th century chancel and 14th century tower. A Brief of 1819 states that the church was "greatly decayed, that the foundation, walls, and roof of the

body are particularly dangerous and necessary to be taken down (leaving the chancel and tower standing) and the same to be rebuilt upon a scale something larger . . ." The cost of this was estimated at £1,194 5s 4d, but this sum could not be raised and the rebuilding had to wait until several years later, when it was carried out by H. Cockbain.

Belper, St Faith

1890 mission church.

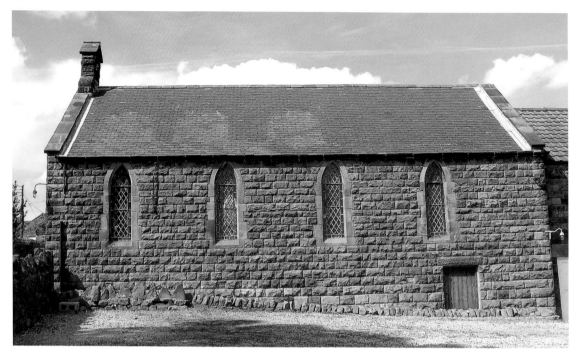

Belper, St Peter

19th century: Perpendicular style

Belper is a corruption of Beaurepaire or Bellerepaire, so named for the beauty of the location, perhaps by Edmund, Earl of Lancaster, son of Henry III. Edmund was lord of the manor and is likely to have founded the original chapel, which was dedicated to John the Baptist.

The present church is 1824 by Habershon, replacing the 13th century St John's chapel which was now too small for the parish which had expanded greatly due to the Industrial Revolution. The tower and east end were repaired in 2002 by A. Short & Partners.

J. C. Cox

The chapel to St John the Baptist, replaced by the present church of St Peter. The chapel is now used as a meeting room and heritage centre.

Belper, Christ Church

19th century: Early English style
Built in 1850 by H.I. Stevens.

Belper, St Swithun

20th century
Built in 1913.

Biggin by Hartington, St Thomas

19th century: Early Gothic style
Built in 1846-8 by H.E. Shellard on a site given by the Duke of Devonshire. This became an ecclesiastical parish in 1849. Previous to the building of this church, the inhabitants of Biggin worshipped in the south transept of Hartington church.

Birchover, St Michael and All Angels

18th century

Also known as the Rowter chapel or the Church of Jesus, this private chapel was built for the Revd Thomas Eyre who died in 1717 and is buried here. Eyre was fascinated with the Rowtor Rocks in this area, which have druidical connections.

The building was neglected and used for storage during the early 19th century but was restored in 1869. A chancel and porch were added at this time and the south windows restored in the Gothic style. Architectural fragments, perhaps from an earlier chapel, were built into the west side of the porch. These had been found in walls in the area and may originate from the original church whose whereabouts is unknown. Pevsner however, suspects that they may actually have been carved by the Revd C.W. Summerfield around 1945. Summerfield certainly is responsible for the elaborate wood carving inside the church. The modern stained glass is by Brian Clarke and dates from the 1970s.

These fragments may be from an earlier chapel, although it is possible that they are Summerfield's work

The 1949 pulpit by Summerfield is consructed from a number of different kinds of wood and was inspired by the book of Ezekiel. The pew ends are also by Summerfield.

Blackwell, St Werburgh

Early English
Of the original church which was given by William FitzRanulph to the Priory of Thurgarten early in the reign of Henry II, only one pillar remains. In 1823, the Archdeacon Butler, declared that the original church should be pulled down and replaced, declaring that "The church has been suffered to go into a state of most ruinous decay. It is unsafe, nay highly dangerous for the parishioners to assemble in it in windy weather, and any attempt at temporary repairs will only subject them to further expense as it is impossible to do it effectively. The parishioners are highly to blame and have nothing but their own neglect to thank." (Cox). After much debate, the order was given in 1824, apparently against the will of the churchwardens who would have preferred to repair the original building. One can only regret that they lost the argument as the brief authorising the rebuilding described the original church as being "believed to be one of the oldest in our county of Derby". The rebuilding was carried out in 1827-18 by Daniel Hodkin and the acrimony over the rebuilding may have carried over into his relationship with the churchwardens as he was not permitted to add his planned pinnacles to the tower. The present tower is 1878, by J.B. Mitchell-Withers. The church was rebuilt again in 1879 and reopened in 1891.

The porch contains the stump of a Saxon cross which was originally in the churchyard and would indicate that this was a place of worship well before the Norman period.

This church is one of only eight in the country dedicated to St Werburgh, princess of Mercia and Abbess of the Convent of Ely who died in 699.

Blagreaves, St Andrew

20th century: Modern
This was originally the church hall for St Peter's, Littleover and was built in the 1950s.

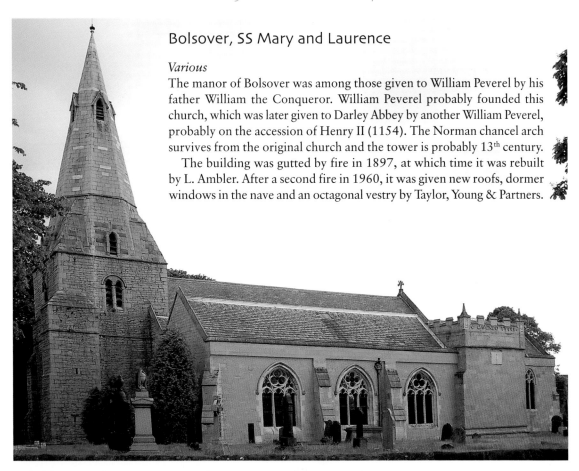

Bolsover, SS Mary and Laurence

Various

The manor of Bolsover was among those given to William Peverel by his father William the Conqueror. William Peverel probably founded this church, which was later given to Darley Abbey by another William Peverel, probably on the accession of Henry II (1154). The Norman chancel arch survives from the original church and the tower is probably 13th century.

The building was gutted by fire in 1897, at which time it was rebuilt by L. Ambler. After a second fire in 1960, it was given new roofs, dormer windows in the nave and an octagonal vestry by Taylor, Young & Partners.

The 1624 Cavendish chapel has survived, as has a late 13th century bas-relief depicting the nativity which may have been used as an altar piece in the original church. Its mutilation may date from the Reformation when it was decreed in 1663 by Parliament that "All Crucifixes, Crosses, and all other Images and Pictures of Saints in any Churches, Chappells or other places of Publick Prayer, shall be taken away and defaced".

by J.C. Cox

Bonsall, St James

Various: Mainly Decorated
At the time of the Domesday Survey, Bonsall was a hamlet of the royal manor of Mestesforde and no church for Bonsall appears in the Survey. The first mention of a church here occurs in the Taxation Roll of Pope Nicholas IV in 1291. By 1310, it was in the hands of Lincoln Cathedral, probably having passed there along with the church at Wirksworth, for which it was a chapel. The building dates back to the 13th century, but the outer walls were largely rebuilt in 1862-3 by Ewan Christian. The tower is 15th century.

The church contains, at the base of one of the pillars, the Bonsall imp – a cross between a frog and a unicorn.

Borrowash, St Stephen

19th century: Early English style
This church by P.H. Currey was opened in 1890. The 18th century wrought-iron screen and communion rail are probably by Bakewell.

Boulton by Derby, St Mary the Virgin

19th and 20th century
This was originally a chapel within the parish of St Peter, Derby, but by the time of the Parliamentary Commissioners in 1650, it had been united to Alvaston, though it was unclear whether it was a chapel or an independent church at this time. It became a benefice in 1730, thanks to the Queen Anne's Bounty.

The building is largely 19th and 20th century with some Norman remnants such as the south doorway and the north chancel doorway. The Norman chancel arch was removed in 1871, at which time the church was enlarged and the bell turret added. The west end is 1840 by John Mason and the church was enlarged in 1960 by Sebastian Comper. The outer doorway of the porch is 13th century.

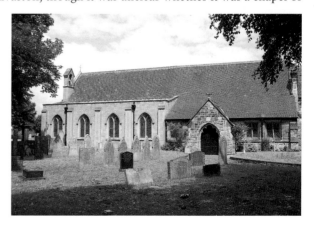

Boylestone, St John the Baptist

Decorated

The earliest reference to a church here is found in a report commissioned by Edward I in 1272. However, the present building is 14th century with a 15th century east window.

Towards the end of May 1644, 200 Royalist soldiers under the command of Colonel Eyre stayed in the church overnight but were ambushed and captured the next morning.

Alterations were made in 1843–44 by H. Duesbury, and the tower with its rather odd roof was added at this time – previous to this, the church had apparently had a square, wooden tower. The church was repaired again in 1981 by Anthony Short & Partners.

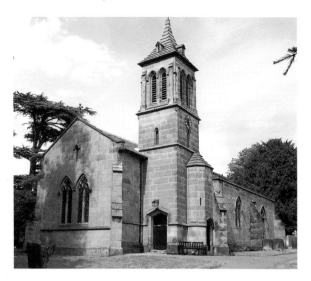

Brackenfield, Holy Trinity

19th century: Decorated style

Originally a chapel of ease for Morton, Brackenfield chapel was built c1500. Brackenfield became a benefice in 1758, but the chapel itself fell into disuse and was replaced by the church built in 1856-7 by T.C. Hine with the northeast chapel and vestry added in 1872. The 15th century screen survives from the original chapel. The chancel was reroofed in 2000, by A.Short & Partners.

Bradbourne, All Saints

Saxon and Norman

Bradbourne already had a church and priest at the time of the Domesday Survey. The manor was held by the Caus family from 1100 and they gave the church with its four chapels (Atlow, Ballidon, Brassington and Tissington) to the Priory of Dunstable in Bedfordshire in 1205. The Norman tower and nave were added to the Saxon church in the early 12th century. The outside north of the church, however, dates back in parts to the early 11th century.

The building was enlarged in the Early English style after 1205 and the Norman doorway was moved to the foot of the tower in the 13th–14th century. The east window dates to c.1320 and the chancel arch is probably 14th century.

The church was repaired in 1938-47 by P.H. Currey and again in 1947-50 by Ogden & Wood.

The cross shaft in the churchyard dates from c800.

The painting on the south wall dates from the 16th / 17th century and shows Ecclesiastes v.1.

Above: The Norman tub font.

The south aisle chapel screen is by Currey & Thompson, 1921.

Bradley, All Saints

14th century

Until the 13th century, Bradley was a chapelry of Ashbourne and thus part of the gift to the Dean of Lincoln. In the Taxation Roll of Pope Nicholas IV (drawn up 1240-1291), Bradley is classified as an independent *ecclesia*.

The Parliamentary Commissioners say of Bradley that it is "a parsonage really worth threescore pounds per annum, noe chappell apperteyning."

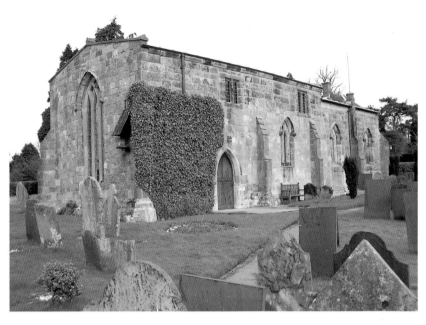

There was probably a Norman building here originally, but the present building is early 14th century, probably dating from 1329-36 when Anthony Beck was Dean of Lincoln. The church seems to have had a steeple – one is mentioned in 1698 – that was later destroyed by lightning. A brick porch, may be seen in Meynell's sketch but this was later removed.

The altar rails are late 17th or late 18th Century. The stone cross in the churchyard was beheaded by Cromwell's soldiers.

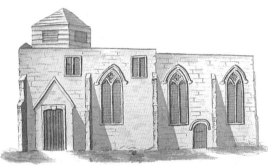

Bradwell, St Barnabas

19th century: Early English style

The church was built in the 1860s by C.C. Townsend The tower was added in 1888–91 by Naylor & Sale. There is a window by Burlison & Grylls in memory of the Revd William James Webb who served here from 1868–1881. The pulpit is made partly from two desks donated by Trinity College, Cambridge.

Until this church was built, the villagers had to attend the church in Hope, though from time to time services were held in the village school. The church became an independent parish in 1875.

Brailsford, All Saints

Brailsford appears in the Domesday Survey as having a priest and half a church. This did not mean that the church was incomplete, but that it was shared with the adjacent manor of Ednaston and was located midway between the two (Ednaston) stood a mile southwest of Brailsford).

The Parliamentary Commissioners of 1650 note that "Mr John Crompton is Incumbent, a man disaffected to the present government".

It seems that the original Norman church was even larger than the present one and there are a number of Norman remnants, including some good Norman pillars inside. There is also the stump of a Saxon cross in the churchyard. The chancel is of the style of the early 14th century and the present tower is c1500. The church was restored in 1863.

The parish registers go back to 1647 – here are two interesting entries:

1699 19th April Churchwardens gathered 22s 9d towards relief of 11,500 protestant Vaudois and French, cruelly turned out of their countrey, and now seeking for a settlement in the territories of the protestant princes in Germany.

1711 April 16th Samuel, son of Thomas Eley, was baptized, aged 16 years, having received only before when an infant the mock baptism of the Presbyterians.

Pew ends by A. R. Poeys, 1913.

Brampton, St Mark

20th century

A hall was built here in 1939 to replace the Lower Brampton Mission which itself had been built in 1894. The hall originally served both as a school and church, but later as a church alone and was replaced by the present building in 1960.

Brampton, St Thomas

19th century: Perpendicular style
This area was part of the parish of Old Brampton until this church, St Thomas at Brampton-over-Moor was dedicated in 1832. It is a Commissioners' building, rebuilt by Joseph Mitchell in 1846-48. A chancel by Naylor and Sale added in 1891. The church underwent a major refurbishment in 1998-99.

Brassington, St James

Norman
This church, which dates from the 11th–12th century, was one of the chapels of Bradbourne given over with it to the Priory of Dunstable. The first documentary mention of it occurs in 1278, but it is clearly much older, being essentially a Norman church, despite much subsequent alteration. The south porch is 13th century and the tower Norman, within which is an ancient stone carving of a man with his hand over his heart. The north aisle in 1879–1881 by F.J. Robinson. The chancel, which is unusual in that it has a small south chancel aisle, was lengthened during the restoration of 1881–1882.

Breadsall, All Saints

Various: Mainly Perpendicular

The Domesday Survey records that Breadsall had a church and a priest. Although there was probably a Saxon church here followed by a Norman one, all that remains of the Norman church is the late Norman south doorway. The whole church would have been reconstructed in the 13th century, but it was much restored by W. D. Caroë (of Caroë & Passmore) in 1915 after it had been set on fire by Suffragettes on 5th June 1914. The 13th century tower has a 14th century spire. The roof was repaired in 1958-9 by Naylor, Sale & Widdows.

J. C. Cox.

The chancel screen is by H. W. Whitaker in 1929 recreation of the medieval screen which had been destroyed in the fire of 1914.

Breaston, St Michael and All Angels

Various: Mainly late early English

With the tower and south aisle dating from early 13th century, this was originally a chapel in the Sawley parish. The church was rebuilt in 1350, when the chancel was lengthened. It was restored in 1871 and then again in 1895 by Evans and Jolley. The font dates from 1720.

Bretby, St Wystan

19th century: Perpendicular

Bretby originated as a chapel of Repton, as mentioned in references to the latter in 1271 and 1279.

The old chapel, which probably dated from the 13th century, was demolished in the mid 1870s and replaced with the present building by T. H. Wyatt, which was opened on the 4th of July 1877.

Brimington, St Michael

19th century

The original chapel was demolished and rebuilt in 1808, keeping only the tower which had been rebuilt at the expense of Joshua Jebb in 1796. The building was again demolished and rebuilt in 1846/1847 by J. Mitchell and the tower was made taller at this time. The chancel, by Naylor & Sale, was added in 1891.

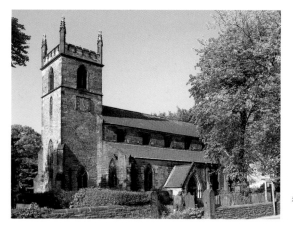

Burbage, Christ Church

19th century: Norman style

Designed by H. Curry in 1860 as part of the development of Buxton by the then Duke of Devonshire, who also donated the land, the church was consecrated on 1st August 1861. The south middle window is by Morris & Co to a design by Burne-Jones.

The church became an ecclesiastical parish in 1869 and underwent an extensive renovation in 1984.

Buxton, St Anne

Mainly 17th century

The origins of this church go back to the Chapel of St Anne at the Holy Wells of Buxton, renowned for their healing powers. Sir William Bassett, visiting the chapel during the Protectorate of Cromwell, wrote indignantly of the crutches and other 'pagan' offerings which had been hung up in the chapel in thanksgiving for healings. He had these torn down and suppressed the further use of the chapel.

The present church was originally dedicated to St John the Evangelist. Although the date over the porch is 1625, the fabric of the building may be much earlier – it may have originated as a barn or may consist of fragments from the earlier chapel. A vestry was added in 1715. The declining condition of the church led the congregation to petition for the building of a new church in 1798, but this was not successful and the congregation transferred to the Assembly Rooms for worship until the church of St John the Baptist was built in 1811. The church was then converted into a school and continued as such (with an intermission of a few years when it was used again as a church) until it became a Sunday School and then a mortuary chapel and eventually fell into disuse.

In 1885, the building was restored and brought back into use as a church. Having been originally dedicated to St John the Evangelist, it was now rededicated to St Anne. The church was restored again in 1956-7.

Top right: The font may be Saxon, despite the date carved on it. The font had been used as a pig trough in the 19th century, until it was restored to its place and rededicated in 1906.

Buxton, St John the Baptist

19th century: Tuscan style

The church now known as St Anne was originally the church of St John the Evangelist and, replacing an earlier chapel, first served as the church for Buxton. By about 1798, this building was falling into disrepair and was proving too small for the growing population. A Brief was applied for to build a new church, but funds were not forthcoming and the congregation moved into the local Assembly Rooms for worship until permission was granted in 1811 to build a new church.

The building of the church, by John White at the expense of the Duke of Devonshire began in 1811 and it was consecrated on 9th August 1812. It was not until1898, however, that it acquired its own parish.

The chancel was formed in 1896-7 by Blomfield & Son out of the east entrance portico. The mosaics in the chancel date from 1902 and the west gallery was added in 1911. Dry rot brought the ceiling very close to collapse in 1937, necessitating its replacement. The church was again renovated in 1973.

Buxton, St Mary

19th century: Arts & Crafts

In 1891 a Miss Mirrlees gave £500 for the provision of a church for the area and to pay for a priest for four years. In 1897, a temporary building was erected, made from timber and galvanised iron – one of what was known as the 'tin churches' of the time. The Duke of Devonshire donated the field next to this for the erection of the permanent stone church which was designed in the Arts and Crafts style in 1914-15 by Currey & Thompson and built by Herbert Robinson. The incumbent, at the time, was Father Currey who was brother of P.H. Currey. The church was dedicated on 16th August 1917.

Buxworth, St James

19th century: Early English
Built in 1874 by J. Lowe.

Caldwell, St Giles

Early English
This is a little Norman chapel, which has been much renewed. The east window is 1913 by Burlison & Grylls.

Calke, St Giles

19th century
There was a priory of canons established at Calke shortly after the Norman Conquest. This was later incorporated with Repton Priory. After the dissolution of the monasteries, Calke Abbey came into the hands of the Crown, which later granted it to the Earl of Warwick.

The original priory was dedicated to St Giles and this dedication was kept for the private chapel of the house, the chapel originally being a parish church in its own right.

The Parliamentary Commissioners say of it : "Calke is a peculiar Sr John Harper of the same Baronett is impropriator and procures the cure supplied. Mr Crossely officiates, is a man disaffected and scandalous and reputed to be sequestered in the countye of Leycester. It lyes neare unto Tycknall and may conveniently be united to Tycknall and the chapel at Calke disused."

The church was rebuilt in 1826 by Sir George Crewe and contains older tombs of the Harpur family. The Norman doorway was still to be seen in 1816 but is now gone. The tracery of the windows is unusual in that the material used is cast iron. The original Early English font remains, having been preserved from the old church.

Calow, St Peter

19th century
The church was built in 1869 by S. Rollinson. The steeple and spire were added in 1887.

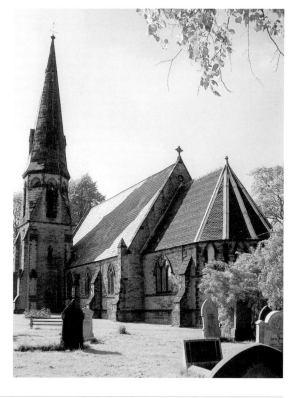

Carsington, St Margaret

Perpendicular
This was a parochial chapelry of Wirksworth Church, and given along with the latter to the Cathedral of Lincoln by Henry I. It had become an *ecclesia* by the time of the Taxation Roll of Pope Nicholas IV in 1291, though the advowson remained in the possession of Lincoln Cathedral.

The 12th century building was completely rebuilt in 1648 in the Gothic style. The sundial on the south wall reads "Re-edified 1648". The west gallery is 1704. The west end was altered in the 19th century with the addition of the bellcote and the south porch. The reredos and altar are 1913 by Currey & Thompson.

Castleton, St Edmund

Various

Although the church is not mentioned in the Domesday Survey, it has Norman features which indicate that it must date from not long after. It is likely that it was built by William Peverel, whose castle overlooks the village. The Peverel family continued to hold the church, castle and surrounding estates until the reign of Henry II when these were forfeited to the crown as a punishment for the poisoning of Ranulph, Earl of Chester.

Of the original Norman building, very little has survived

the extensive rebuilding and restorations of later years, although the chancel arch, which matches an arch in the castle wall, is still intact in its original form. The tower is late Perpendicular, and the ceiling is 17th century, as are the box pews with the names of their owners.

St Edmund was the King of East Anglia, martyred in 869 AD.

The pews were restored in 1977-80, and a new vestery added in 1988.

Chaddesden, St Mary

Decorated
This was one of the chapelries of Spondon and is mentioned in a document of 1347 in which the chapel was granted rights of burial. This was applied for on account of the distance from Spondon and was granted on condition that the fees in such cases should still go to the vicar of the mother church. A chantry was founded here in 1357 by Henry Chaddesden.

The impressive chancel is reached through a 15th century rood screen. The high altar triptych is by Walter Tapper (1904). The church was restored in 1859 by Street and G. Place, at which time the roofs were raised to their present high pitch. The east window and the east window of the north aisle were badly damaged by a bomb in the Second World War.

Chaddesden, St Philip

20th century: Gothic (simplified)
Built in 1954-6 by Milburn & Partners of concrete reinforced stone.

Chapel-en-le-Frith, St Thomas á Becket

Various

Chapel-en-le-Frith means Chapel in the Forest and the church was founded in 1225 by the foresters of the Royal Forest of the High Peak. Originally a chapel of ease, it became a church in 1317 due to the expansion of the town. Parts of the foundations, the lower sections of the walls and the piscina by the Communion table probably date from the original building, but the rest is largely 14th century. There is a Saxon cross shaft in the churchyard indicating that there may have been a church here prior to the foresters' chapel.

The south porch, south aisle and tower were rebuilt in 1731-33 in the classical style by G. Platt. The chancel was much altered and restored in 1890-3 by Darbyshire & Smith. The Revd William Bagshawe, known as the "Apostle of the Peak", is buried in the chancel.

A forester's grave, showing his axe and initials

The church was used as a prison in 1648 for 1,500 prisoners following the battle at Ribblesdale Moor – as recorded in the church registers:

"1648 Sept 11. There came to this town of Scots army led by the Duke of Hambleton, and squandered by Colonel Lord Cromwell, sent hither prisoners from Stopford under the conduct of Marshall Edward Matthews, said to be 1500 in number put into ye church Sept 14. They went away Sept 30 following. There were buried of them before the rest went away 44 persons, and more buried Oct.2 who were not able to march, and the same yt died by the way before they came to Cheshire 10 and more." (from the Reliquary vol.6.)

The box pews date from 1834. The original tie beam roof was revealed during the 1890 restoration. The Flemish chandelier in the nave was given to the church in 1731. The window to the east of the north aisle (to the left of the picture) is by David Pilkington and Steven Parsons and dates from the 1990s.

Charlesworth, St John the Evangelist

19th century: Early English style
It seems that a chapel dedicated to St Mary Magdalene was built here c1308 by Basingwerk Abbey, but this eventually fell into disuse and disrepair after the dissolution of the monasteries. It passed into the hands of a Presbyterian congregation and was completely rebuilt c1797. A new Church of England church by J. Mitchell was built here in 1848-9. Its roof was replaced in 1853 following storm damage.

Chellaston, St Peter

Decorated
This was held by the bishop of Carlisle in conjunction with Melbourne and, although not a chapel of the latter, its chaplain was appointed by the Rector of Melbourne. By 1650, according to the Parliamentary Commissioners, it was: ". . . a small parish that hath a glebe and vicarall Tythes (. . .) it lyes not farre distant from Swarkestone and may be conveniently be united thereunto. Mr John Endon serves the cure of noe good repute".

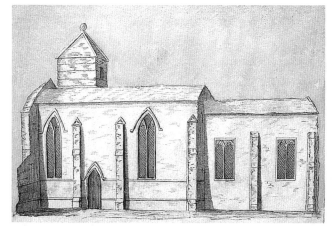

The font is Norman with a base from the Decorated period and the window tracery is 13th century. Other parts date from the 14th century and later. The church was repaired and the west tower was rebuilt in 1841-2 by John Mason and the church restored in 1884. The church was repaired again in 1926-7 by Currey & Thompson.

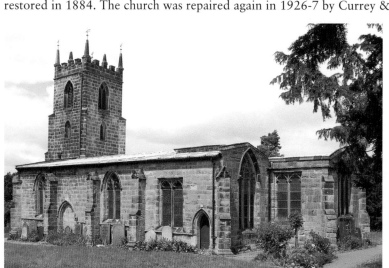

Chelmorton and Flagg, St John the Baptist

Mainly Decorated

The first written mention of a chapel at Chelmorton occurs in 1256, although a church may have existed here earlier. The chapel was made into a parish church around 1650.

There was probably a Norman building originally on this site, which would have been rebuilt in the 13th century. The south transept is very large and may have been intended as the chantry for which permission was given in 1256. The chancel, which was rebuilt in the late 15th century, is according to Cox, a very good example of late Perpendicular style. The spire, too, is 15th century.

The Saxon coffin lids in the porch.

The nave, chancel and south transept are 13th and 14th century. The south arcade, however, is probably c1200. The stone rood screen dates from1345 and has a 20th century wooden top section. The Elizabethan porch is made from coffin lids. At 1,200 ft above sea level, this is said to be the highest church in Derbyshire and is built into sloping ground, which meant that it was notable, prior to its 19th century restoration (in 1868-75 by H. Currey and J.D. Simpson), for the differences in level between the various parts of the church. It was described then as having a chancel "five feet, more or less, higher than the entrance to the south door".

There were frescoes in the south transept, probably dating from the time of James I.

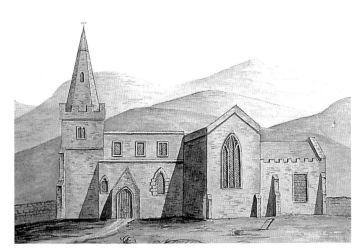

Chesterfield, St Mary and All Saints

Decorated

Built near the site of a Roman fort held here until the 2nd century, this church is famous for its bizarrely twisted spire – a result of the warping of the lead and wood of which it was constructed sometime between 1350 and 1370. The church was given to the Dean and Chapter of Lincoln by William Rufus (d.1110). Nothing now remains of the original Norman church, which was replaced by the present one, probably around 1250. The present structure is largely 14th century, with a west door and east window that were added at the time of its restoration in 1843 by Gilbert Scott. Earlier, in 1817, there had been something of a panic, concerning the stability of the spire – various architectural advisors declared it to be in imminent danger of collapse. Plans were made for its demolition and replacement with a stone spire, but local inhabitants objected to this and the spire was kept after a few repairs were made. The tower and spire also underwent repairs in 1933-34 by Moore & Moore. The church was restored in 1843 by Scott & Moffatt.

Unusually for an English church, it has a large number of chapels, due to the multiplicity of local guilds. The church also contains a number of significant monuments, including a shrouded memorial, one of only two in Derbyshire (the other being at Fenny Bentley).

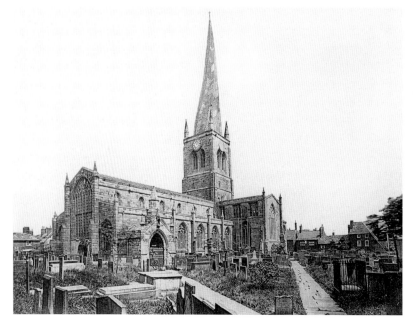

J. C. Cox

Left: The pulpit is a fine example of fine Jacobean work.

Above: The High Altar is by Temple Moore, and the 1953 east window is by Christopher Webb.

This monument with shrouded figure is uninscribed. The only other depiction in Derbyshire of such a shrouded figure is the Beresford tomb in Fenny Bentley church.

Chesterfield, SS Augustine

20th century: Lombard Romanesque style.
Built in 1931 by Hicks & Charlewood. The stained glass in the south chapel is by Nuttgens in 1959. Three bays and a baptistery were added to the nave in 1949-51 by G.E. Charlewood.
The dedication is to two Saints Augustine – Augustine of Hippo and Augustine of Canterbury.

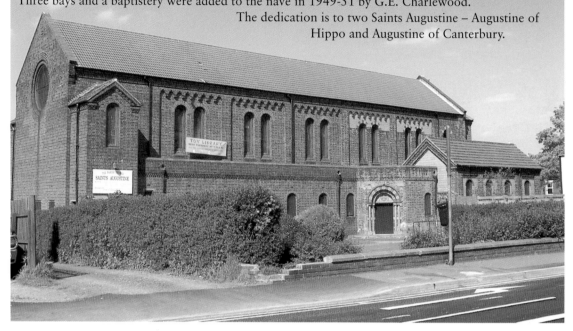

Chesterfield, Christ Church

19th century: Early English style
Built in 1869 by S. Rollinson with north and south aisles added in 1913-14 by Rollinson & Sons. At this time the nave was also extended westwards.

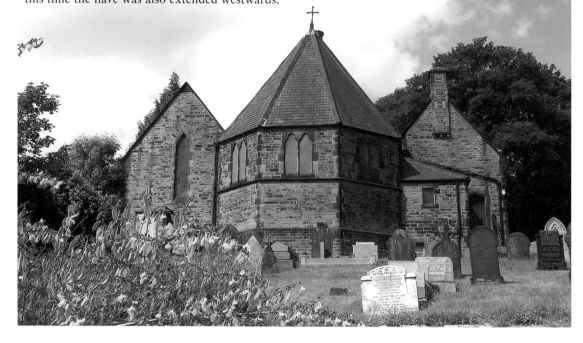

Chesterfield, Holy Trinity

19th century: Early English style
Built in 1838 by Thomas Johnson, the church was altered in 1888 – 1889 by S. Rollinson. The 1848 east window is in memory of the engineer George Stephenson who is buried in the church.

Chinley, St Mary

Early 20th century
Built in 1907 with an extension by J.B. Blagney in 1957 – 72

Church Broughton, St Michael and All Angels

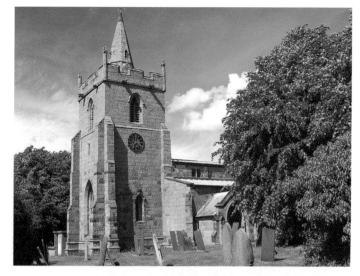

Mainly 14th century: Decorated

The church was founded in the 12th century, although there are traces of an earlier Norman building. It may have been built by the Priory of Tutbury, to whom the manor of Broughton was given by Henry de Ferrers in the reign of William the Conqueror.

The present structure is mostly 14th century. It is in the Decorated style, with the nave raised to allow for a clerestory in the Perpendicular period. W.H. Auden's uncle and cousin were vicars of this parish and he is known to have stayed here.

The church registers are very well preserved and Cox gives the following extract:

"1767 May, daughter of Humphrey Morley, was born and baptised June 2nd. N.B. This child had two teeth cut, when born. I saw the teeth when they brought the child to me to baptise it.

Jno. Dimott, Vicar"

J. C. Cox

Right: The Norman font

Clay Cross, St Bartholomew

19ᵗʰ century: Early English style
Built in 1851 by H.I. Stevens with the 70 ft spire added in 1856. The south aisle window is 1879 by Morris & Co. The base of the cross after which the town is named is in the churchyard. The church was repaired in 1986 and the roof renewed in 1999. Church rooms were added in the early 1990s and a reordering was carried out in 2003, both by A. Short & Partners.

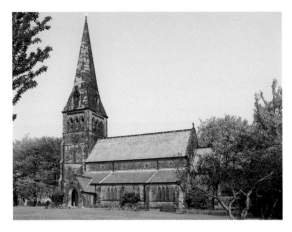

Clifton, Holy Trinity

19ᵗʰ century: Early English style
There was originally a chapel of ease here for Ashbourne. This became derelict and was demolished c1750 and its stones used in the repairs being made to St Oswald's church. The present building by H.I. Stevens dates from 1845. The apse and the bell-tower are by Slater & Carpenter and were added in 1868.

Clowne, St John the Baptist

Early English style
The church first appears in the historical records during the reign of Henry III (1216-1272) in a reference to a church of All Saints at Clowne. However the dedication was later changed to St John the Baptist, as frequently happened when a church was rebuilt. The porch was added in 1720. There is still a Norman nave and chancel arch and the Norman chancel was rebuilt in 1955.

Codnor, St James

19ᵗʰ century: Early English style
Commissioners' church by R. Barber, this dates from 1843-44. The chancel, by J. Holden was added 1888-90. The font was found in the precincts of Codnor castle and had been used at one point as a pig trough.

Cotmanhay and Shipley, Christ Church

20th century
The original church was built in 1847-8 by H.I. Stevens in the Early English style at a cost of £2,600 on a site donated by the Duke of Rutland. This was replaced by the present Worship Centre by Graham Weston in 1988.

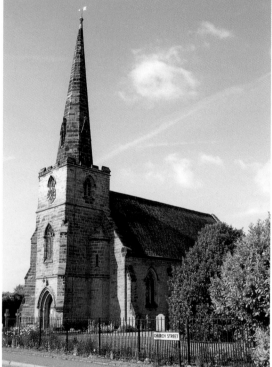

Coton in the Elms, St Mary

19th century
This was probably the chapel appertaining to Lullington which was mentioned in Lullington's entry in the Taxation Roll of 1291.

The original church was demolished shortly after the Reformation, though there may still have been a chapel at Coton in 1603. The present building, by H.I. Stevens, dates from 1844-6. The church became an ecclesiastical parish in 1866.

Cressbrook, St John the Evangelist

19th century
Built in 1877 by H. Cockbain as part of the model village for the workers at the Cressbrook Mill in the Wye valley. The furnishings were carved by Advent Hunstone.

Cresswell, St Mary Magdalene

19th century
Built in 1899- 1900 by L. Ambler for the Duke of Portland. Ambler also added the aisles in 1914, and the tower in 1927. It contains a memorial window to the 1950 Cresswell Colliery disaster.

Crich, St Mary

Decorated
The church is not mentioned in the Domesday Survey, but it does date from not long after (probably 1135), as can be seen from the Norman font and arches. The chancel is 14th century and contains a rare built-in stone bible rest. The tower and spire dates from the same period. The roof was replaced in 1860-61 by Benjamin Ferrey and the church restored by H. Currey.

Below: A rare stone bible rest.

Above: A beam from the original church. The inscription is particularly interesting in that the incumbent is described as a minister rather than a priest – a reflection of the strongly protestant ethos of the time, 1649, in which the inscription was made.

Cromford, St Mary

19th century

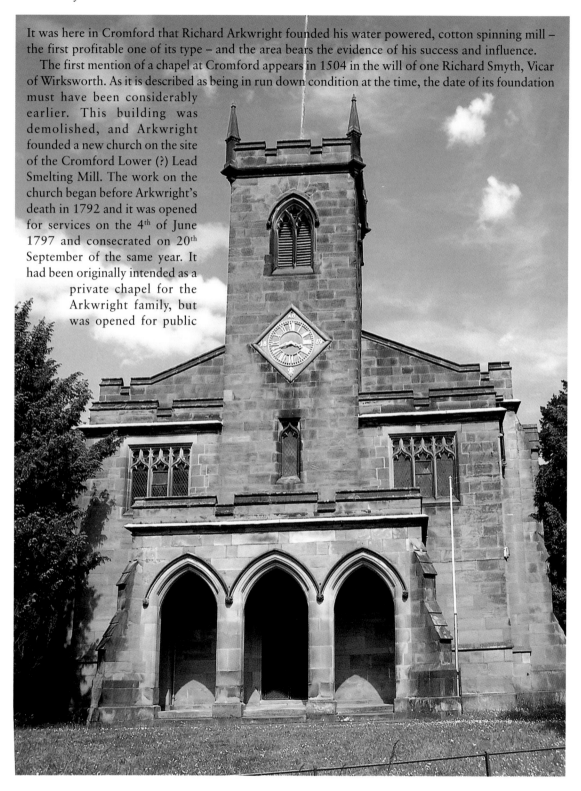

It was here in Cromford that Richard Arkwright founded his water powered, cotton spinning mill – the first profitable one of its type – and the area bears the evidence of his success and influence.

The first mention of a chapel at Cromford appears in 1504 in the will of one Richard Smyth, Vicar of Wirksworth. As it is described as being in run down condition at the time, the date of its foundation must have been considerably earlier. This building was demolished, and Arkwright founded a new church on the site of the Cromford Lower (?) Lead Smelting Mill. The work on the church began before Arkwright's death in 1792 and it was opened for services on the 4th of June 1797 and consecrated on 20th September of the same year. It had been originally intended as a private chapel for the Arkwright family, but was opened for public use by Arkwright's son Richard. It became an ecclesiastical parish in 1869.

The church was gothicised in 1858 by H.I. Stevens through an enlargement of the chancel arch, extension of the chancel, remodelling of the windows and the addition of a porch and tower to what had been previously a small, boxy building. The apsidal chancel was added at a later date.

In honour of the church's centenary and Queen Victoria's Diamond Jubilee, the east windows and murals were begun by Alfred Octavius Hemmings of London. The

Chancel

Chancel south wall

paintings were completed by the start of the 1900s, but many were lost by the 1970s as a result of damage from damp and other environmental problems. The church was reroofed in 1996 with stainless steel and monitoring was undertaken to stabilise the interior environment. Once this stability was achieved, work began, by the Wall Paintings Workshop of Faversham, to restore the paintings. Those that had survived were restored and those which had vanished altogether were recreated from the photographic records. The restoration was recently completed and the paintings are visible again in all their glory.

Nave north wall

Croxall cum Oakley, St John the Baptist

14th century

The advowson of the church at Croxall was given to Repton Priory in 1239. The Parliamentary Commissioners of 1650 say that Croxall is: "really worth nine and fortye pounds six shillings and sixpence per annum. Mr John Hough is viccar and of noe good repute. Mr Hinglye is curate, a man of good repute."

The church is largely 14th century, restored and repaired in 1854.

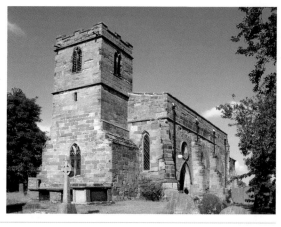

Cubley, St Andrew

Mainly Decorated

The Domesday Survey records that Cubley had a priest and a church, and there are some good Norman remains in the church as well as a Norman font, and there are some fragments in the north wall of the nave which are possibly Saxon in origin. The south arcade is late 12th century and the chancel is 13th century. The chancel was repaired in 1845.

The tower was built during the reign of Henry VIII and was restored in 1874 by St Aubyn.

In the early 19th century, the south porch was taken down and blocked up, leaving only the small chancel door as an entrance. The 1874 alterations, however, restored the porch and its proper function.

Left: The east window is by Burlison & Grylls, 1874

Curbar, All Saints

19th century: Early English style
This was built in 1868 by Anthony Salvin
and consecrated 26th May 1868.

Dalbury, All Saints

Early English
The Domesday Survey shows Dalbury as having a
church and a priest. No trace remains of that original
church, although there is a font which may be of an
early date.

The church largely dates from the 13th century,
but was extensively repaired in 1629. It was enlarged
and altered with a north aisle in 1844.

As with many of the older
churches, the porch shows the
marks of arrow sharpening,
dating from the time of
compulsory archery practice on
Sundays!

The 12th century stained glass
of St Michael is probably the
oldest in Derbyshire and has
been restored by the York
Glaziers' Trust.

The woodwork, including this
font cover, is mainly by the Revd
Charles Cotton who was Rector
at this time. His arms appear on
the bosses of the timbers in the
roof which were put in at this
time to replace the old ones.

Dale Abbey, All Saints

Various

This tiny 25 by 26ft chapel dates from the 12th century and may have been the infirmary chapel for the Abbey of St Mary, of which nothing now remains save the east window and a few fragments. It is attached to a domestic dwelling which was originally the Abbey infirmary then later village inn (during which time the bar was used as a vestry) and subsequently a farmhouse.

The building is of Norman origin and was altered in 1480. The furnishings are 17th century and the whole was rebuilt in 1883.

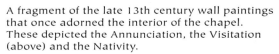
A fragment of the late 13th century wall paintings that once adorned the interior of the chapel. These depicted the Annunciation, the Visitation (above) and the Nativity.

The pulpit dates from 1634

The gallery

Danesmoor, St Barnabas

19th century
A chapel in the North Wingfield parish,
this church was built in 1861.

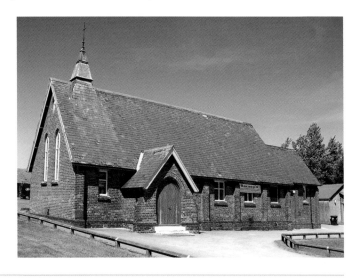

Darley, St Helen

Decorated
Darley is recorded in the Domesday Survey
as having a church and priest. It soon passed
into the hands of the Dean and Chapter of
Lincoln.

The present cruciform church mostly dates
from the 13th century though it has many 15th
century additions. It was restored in 1854 and
enlarged by H.I. Stevens when it was extended
west, the north and south aisles being enlarged
and a new west gallery added.

Nothing remains of the original Saxon
structure and there are only fragments from
the Norman period – such as the
Norman doorway in the south of the
chancel. The north and south windows
date from around 1330.

Coffin lids in the porch

The yew tree in the churchyard
has a circumference of 33 ft
and is possibly the largest in
England.

A Norman fragment in the porch

Darley Abbey, St Matthew

19th century
Originally a chapel of east for St Alkmund's in Derby, this church by Moses Wood was built in 1818-9. It was financed by Walter Evans, on whose birthday on 24th June 1819, the church was consecrated. The chancel was extended during the 1885 alterations and the church was restored and enlarged with a community room in the mid 20th century.

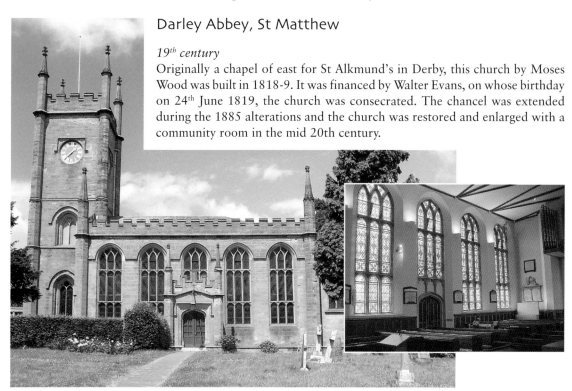

Denby, St Mary the Virgin

Early English
This church started out as a parochial chapelry of Horsley, with the vicar of Horsley providing a priest to carry out the services at Denby. A grant of £200 from Queen Anne's Bounty, along with another £200 from the will of Jane Massie, enabled the church to be changed from a simple cure to a perpetual curacy, so making it more independent from Horsley, an independence which was completed with the later Parliamentary Grant which enabled it to become a full vicarage.

A description of the church in 1825 records a Saxon arcade, but this appears to have been obliterated during the rebuilding and renovations of 1838 during which time the church was enlarged. The chancel and tower are 14th and the clerestory was added in the 15th century. There is also a Norman south arcade. A gallery was added to the north arcade in 1838 and the building was restored in 1902-3 by J. Oldrid Scott. The spire was struck by lightning in 1852.

Derby, SS Alkmund & Werburgh

20th century

This was one of the eight churches in England dedicated to St Alkmund and was built to house his relics. The original Saxon church had been enlarged in the 12th to 15th centuries and here a 9th century sarcophagus had been found. The sarcophagus, perhaps that of St Alkmund himself, is now in the Derby Museum and Art Gallery. The church came into the hands of the Dean and Chapter of Lincoln as part of the College of

All Saints. The ancient church was replaced in 1846 with a church at Bridge Gate by H. I. Stevens. This was, in turn demolished in 1967 to make way for the inner ring road and the present church by Naylor, Sale & Widdows was built in 1967-72 to replace it.

The present church contains the 14th century font from the original building and the alabaster effigy of John Bullock who died 1667. Beneath the fibreglass spire is also a stone which may have been part of St Alkmund's shrine.

Alkmund was the son of King Alured of Northumbria and was martyred in 800AD at the hands of King Eardulph.

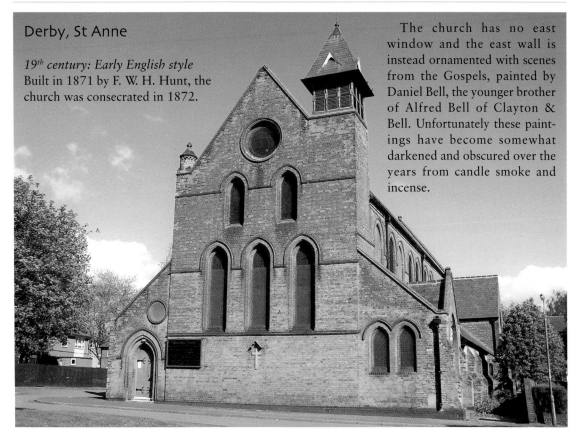

Derby, St Anne

19th century: Early English style
Built in 1871 by F. W. H. Hunt, the church was consecrated in 1872.

The church has no east window and the east wall is instead ornamented with scenes from the Gospels, painted by Daniel Bell, the younger brother of Alfred Bell of Clayton & Bell. Unfortunately these paintings have become somewhat darkened and obscured over the years from candle smoke and incense.

Derby, St Andrew with St Osmund, see Wilmorton on page 187.

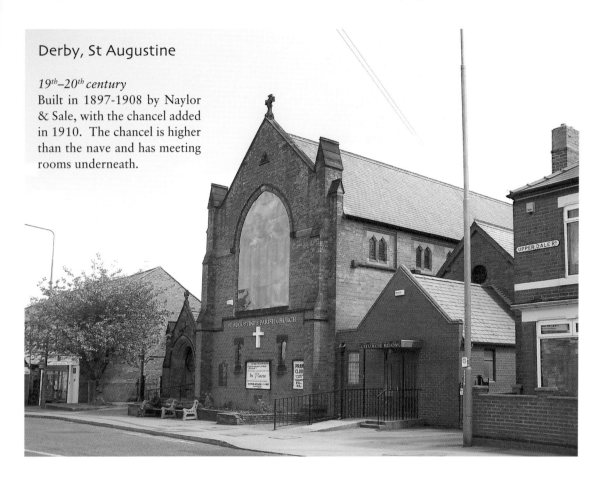

Derby, St Augustine

19th–20th century
Built in 1897-1908 by Naylor
& Sale, with the chancel added
in 1910. The chancel is higher
than the nave and has meeting
rooms underneath.

Derby, St Barnabas

19th century
The 1880 church by A. Coke-Hill
was originally designed as a much
more ambitious project with
transepts and a tower with spire.
However, the original plan was
never carried out to its full extent
and the present building has only a
truncated tower with tiny bellcote.

Coke-Hill is also responsible for
the chancel, apse and vestry added
in 1903. Like St Augustine's above,
it contains meeting rooms under the
chancel.

Derby, St Bartholomew

20th Century: Arts & Crafts
1927 by Currey & Thompson. The apse and vestry, by Humphrey & Hurst, were added in 1966-9.

Derby, St John the Evangelist

19th century: Perpendicular style
Originally a chapel of ease to the now redundant St Werburgh, this 1826-7 Commissioners' Church by Francis Goodwin was designed in imitation of the buildings at Cambridge. It cost nearly £7,500 and was paid for partially by the parliamentary funds and partly by local subscription. The chancel by W.G. Giles was added in 1871, a year after St John's had become a parish church in its own right. In 1891, the church underwent major improvements as well as being reseated and repewed. The west window dates from that time. The gothic windows have cast iron tracery and the heavy corner pinnacles were originally almost twice their present height – they were reduced in 1901 when they were found to be unsafe.

Derby, Cathedral Church of All Saints

Various

This was originally a collegiate church, having 7 to 8 prebendaries and is mentioned in the Domesday Book as having 7 clerks.

Though the foundation of the church is pre-Conquest, the oldest part of the present structure is the 16th century tower. The rest of the church was rebuilt in 1723-5 by James Gibbs in a Roman Doric style in local freestone (a very fine grained stone, it can be cut in any direction). This rebuilding was instigated by the energetic and autocratic Dr Hutchinson who, when a previous project to repair the church fell through, had the entire church (apart from the tower) demolished in the course of one night in February 1723, rather to the horror of the local inhabitants. Hutchinson then set about raising funds for the new building, becoming notorious for his insistent and tireless methods. The style of architecture chosen did not by any means meet with unqualified approval. Black's Guide (1843) says of it:

"Nothing could be more out of character with the medieval tower, than is the general body of the church, and few towns can boast so perfect a specimen of the bad taste of the last century as a first glance at All Saints reveals."

The church was reopened for worship on 25th November 1725, on which occasion a sermon was preached by Dr Hutchinson on the text of Psalm 122: "I was glad when they said unto me, Let us go into the house of the Lord". He may well have been glad, but he did not last much longer in his post and was eventually made to leave town altogether in 1728.

In the 19th century the church was used for secular as well as religious purposes – the corporations would meet here to choose a mayor and parish meetings would be held in the north aisle.

The church was elevated to cathedral status in 1927 with the formation of the new diocese of Derby.

Wrought iron screen by Robert Bakewell.

The colour scheme is by Anthony New 1972.

Alabaster slab c1480 to sub-dean Lawe.

St Katherine's chapel, donated by the local Freemasons in 1973. This area was originally part of the Cavendish famliy vault.

Opposite page: The east view of the church shows clearly its three different stages, the 16th century tower, the James Gibbs chancel and the retro-choir by Sebastian Comper which was added in 1972.

This c1527 wooden monument is a very rare example of its kind.

Derby, St Luke

19th century: Early English/Decorated style
Built in 1872 by Stevens & Robinson, to replace a previous 1868 wooden structure, this is thought to be Robinson's best work. The church was consecrated on the 24th June 1871.

Derby, St Mark

20th century: Arts and Crafts
1938 Arts and Crafts church by Naylor, Sale & Woore. It was built with handmade bricks and tiles, as well as pre-stressed concrete.

Derby, St Mary on the Bridge

14th century bridge chapel (of these only 6 remain in England). The arch of the original bridge can still be seen at the east end. It was turned to secular use after the Reformation, but then reopened as a mission church for St Alkmund's in 1873. It was restored in 1929–30 by Currey & Thompson.

Derby, St Paul

19th century
This church by Barry & Brown was built in 1849. The aisle was added in 1897 by P.H. Currey.

Derby, St Peter and Christ Church with Holy Trinity

Mainly Decorated

By the time of the Domesday Survey, this church was in the hands of Ralph Fitzhurbert, although it was already in existence at the time of Edward the Confessor. The church was given to Darley Abbey by Hugh, dean of All Saints, Derby. A chantry to the Virgin Mary was founded in here in 1338 and another to S. Nicholas in 1348. Most of the church is from an early 14th century rebuilding, making this the only medieval church remaining in the city of Derby. It underwent a major rebuilding during the time of Henry VII (1485–1509) during which, among other things, the nave was raised to accommodate a new clerestory. The tower was rebuilt at this time and the chancel shortened.

The parish rooms at the west end were added in 1972

The screen at the back of the church was donated in 1957 by the Revd C. A. Shaw

The tower was badly damaged in an 1811 earthquake, leading to changes and rebuilding in 1898, when the nave, whose east wall is Norman, was lengthened, and the tower was rebuilt further west. Parish rooms were added at the west end in 1972. The chancel was restored by G.G. Place in 1851-3, and the rest of the church by G.E. Street in 1859.

Glover recounts the following episode from its history:

"Robert Liversage, a dyer, of Derby founded a chapel in this chuch in 1530, and ordered divine service to be celebrated every Friday. Thirteen poor men and women were to be present, each to be rewarded with a silver penny; as much in those days as would support a frugal person. The porches, like those of Bethesda, were crowded with people, who waited for the moving of the doors, as the others for that of the water. While the spiritual sergeant beat up for volunteers at a penny advance, recruits would never be wanting. A sufficient congregation was not doubted; nor their quarrelling for the money. The priest frequently found his hearers in that disorder which his prayers could not rectify; they frequently fought, but not the good fight of faith; nor did ill neighbourhood end with Friday. The hearers used to pay the preacher, but here the case was reversed . . ."

Derby, St Thomas

19th century: Norman Style
The church, by J. Peacock, was consecrated in 1881. The east window is by Mayer of Munich and dates from that time.

Dethick, Christ Church

Decorated

This manor chapel was founded in 1279 by Geoffrey Dethick and was originally dedicated to John the Baptist. Building may have started 50 years earlier, when a licence for the chapel was given by the bishop in 1228 – some of the older parts of the wall do seem to date from then.

Two of the original lancet windows still survive from the original building. The church was restored after a fire in 1872, at which time the timber roof was replaced.

The manor was owned by the Babington family by the 15th century and the chapel was improved in 1530-32 by Anthony Babington. The Perpendicular clerestory and tower were added at this time. Anthony Babington was executed in 1586 for his part in a plot to rescue Mary, Queen of Scots from Wingfield Manor. He had previously made the estate over to his brother George to avoid it being confiscated by the Crown, should the conspiracy fail.

Below the bell openings in the tower can be seen a frieze of the heraldic shields of the families with which the Babingtons had intermarried, most notably the Ferrers, Rollastons and Fitzherberts.

Dethick may get its name from "death oak" suggesting that this was a place of execution at some point.

J.C. Cox

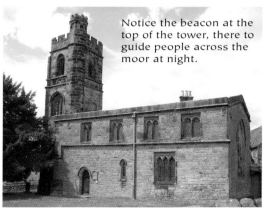

Notice the beacon at the top of the tower, there to guide people across the moor at night.

Dinting Vale, Holy Trinity

19th century: Early English style
Built in 1873–1875 by Mills & Murgatroyd and consecrated on 31st July 1875.

Dove Holes, St Paul

19th century
1878

Doveridge, St Cuthbert

Early English style
Doveridge had a church and a priest at the time of the Domesday Survey. It was given to the priory of Tutbury by Lady Bertha, the wife of Henry de Ferrers. A chantry chapel to the Virgin Mary was founded here in 1392 by the vicar Robert Kniveton. Of the original church, nothing remains. The present building dates from the 13th century. The chancel is a fine example of its kind and still possesses its original lancet windows. The aisles are 14th century and many other alterations were made during the 15th century. The church was repaired and repewed in 1840 and restored in 1869. It also had an octagonal meeting room by D. B. Carton added in the 20th century.

One of the most distinctive features of this church is the 'tunnel' formed by the branches of its ancient yew tree (said to be over 1,000 years old) which provides the approach to the building.

The dedication probably relates to a well of St Cuthbert near the church and Cox notes that there was a tradition that "the parson of Doveridge went over to Tutbury to perform the marriage of Robin Hood."

Draycott, St Mary

19th century

Originally a Wesleyan chapel, this was built in 1832 and a chancel was added later. The building became an Anglican church in 1966.

Dronfield, St John the Baptist

Decorated

The church is first mentioned in the reign of Edward I, when Sir Henry de Brailsford gave the advowson to the Abbey of Beauchief. The Norman church was transformed in 14th and 15th centuries. The chancel is 14th century but was ruined after the Reformation and later restored. The trefoil openings at the clerestory level were added when the church was renewed in 1855. There is also an unusual two storey vestry, the upper floor of which would probably have been for the use of the deacon.

In 1563, a report on the condition of the chancel stated that:

"they say that the said great window and roof of the said chauncell was in decay at the time of the suppression of the said Howse and monastery of Beawchief, and that since that time the same have grown worse, more and more in decay and ruin, and that the cause of the ruin and decay thereof was by reason of the great force, vehemence, and violence of wind and weather; and they also say that the cause of the decay of the glass of the other windows of the said chauncell was by reason that the crows and other vermyne have and do daily use and haunt the said chauncell, for that the said great window is now so in decay." (Cox)

The church was repaired and reseated in 1853-56 by Flockton & Sons.

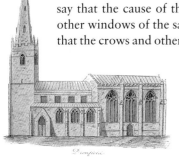

Duckmanton, SS Peter and Paul

17th century

The earliest vicar here was W. de Bollesovre, followed by Robert de Carleton in 1310. In 1558, Sir Francis Leake, patron of the parishes of Sutton and Duckmanton, applied for episcopal sanction for the two parishes to be united. This was obtained on 20th February 1558, and the Duckmanton parishioners were thus instructed to start attending Sutton church instead.

The original church was pulled down at this time. Richard Arkwright later erected a parish room on that site, which is now the parish church.

Duffield, St Alkmund

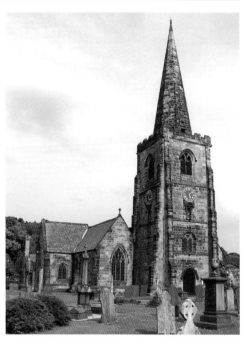

Decorated

The manor of Duffield already had a church and a priest by the time of the Domesday Survey and was given to Henry de Ferrers, along with another 113 manors, by William the Conqueror. There are no traces of the Saxon building – perhaps because it was, like many of the time, a wooden structure. However there are remains of a Norman successor. In 1650, the Parliamentary Commissioners state that: "Duffield is a viccaridge and hath divers hamlets and severall Chappels apperteyning. Mr John Taylor is viccar an able preacher and of good conversation."

The church was extended in the 12th century, but much of the building is 13th and 14th century. It was repaired sometime in 1620-49, according to the parish registers, and again in c1673 on account of it being "much decayed by reason of a late violent flood".

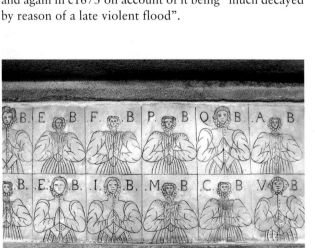

A second restoration followed in 1846 by St Aubyn, at which time the roofs of the north and south aisles were raised and given their present high pitch. It was restored in 1896 by J. O. Scott. A south cloister, connecting the church with the church hall, was added in 1992.

The impressive monument to Anthony Bradshaw, d.1614, his two wives and twenty children.

Earl Sterndale, St Michael and All Angels

19th century
The first mention of a church at Earl Sterndale occurs in the reign of Edward VI. It was a chapel of Hartington and in 1650, the Parliamentary Commissioners recommended that it be made a parish in its own right. However, this did not happen until later, in the Victorian period.

A Brief was obtained in 1819 for the church to be rebuilt as it was "a very ancient structure, and, through length of time greatly decayed . . . and so ruinous that the inhabitants cannot assemble therein . . . without great danger."

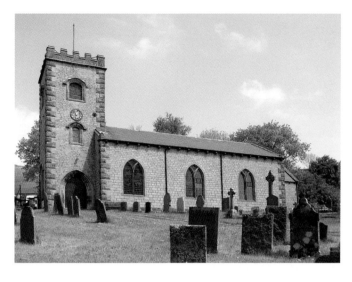

However, the necessary sum of £1700 could not be raised and a second attempt was made in 1824. The building was at last taken down in 1828, having reached a very dilapidated condition indeed and was replaced by the present structure by G.E. Hamilton in 1828-9. The chancel by R.R. Duke was added in 1877. It became the only church in Derbyshire to be seriously damaged by enemy action in the Second World War when, on the night of 9th June 1941, it was hit by incendiary bombs. It was re-roofed and refurbished in 1950-2 by Naylor, Sale & Widdows. The font is probably early 12th century.

Eckington, SS Peter and Paul

Early English
The Domesday Survey mentions a priest here but no church. However, this must be an oversight as the church, which is an important example of 12th and 13th century architectural styles in Derbyshire, was first mentioned in 1002 in the will of Wulfric Spott. The interior arcades are Norman, the east ends of which are earlier.

J. C. Cox

The doorway of the west tower is also Norman, and the spire is 14th century. The south aisle wall and porch are 18th century. The church contains a number of Sitwell monuments.

The building was enlarged and a gallery added by Woodhead & Hurst in 1831-34. The latter suffered a "near fatal accident" in the course of the work. The church was re-gothicised in 1907 by Currey & Thompson.

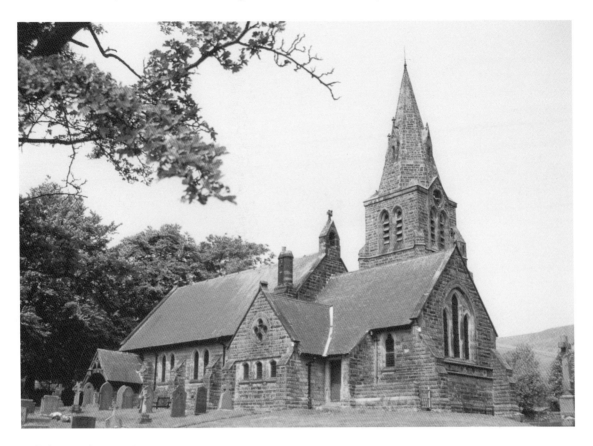

Edale, Holy Trinity

19th century: Early English style

Edale formed part of the parish of Castleton and there was no chapel here until one was built in 1633. In 1795, a Brief was granted to take down this chapel, which was "greatly decayed in every part and much too small". However, the necessary funds could not be raised, and it was not until 1812 that it was replaced by a plain building then replaced again with the present church by William Dawes of Manchester which was completed in 1889. It has stained glass by Comper.

The tower and spire were repaired in 1947-1948 by Whitaker, Glossop & Greaves.

Edensor, St Peter

19th century: Decorated

A Norman church was built in the manor of Edensor shortly after the Domesday Survey, the manor forming part of the estates of Henry de Ferrers. By 1650, the advowson was in the possession of the Earl of Devonshire.

This original church was demolished and rebuilt in 1867 to a design by Sir George Gilbert Scott. Many elements of the earlier structure were incorporated, such as the Norman pillars and the roundheaded doorway in the south porch. It has an Early English interior, tower and spire and the south porch is 15th century, preserved from the old building with its gargoyle and angel.

Kathleen, the sister of President Kennedy, who died in a plane crash, is buried here. There is a plaque in the church commemorating the President's visit.

Above: The church is notable for the 17th century monument to William, 1st Earl of Devonshire, d.1625, and Henry Cavendish, d.1616, preserved from the earlier building. William is shown as a shrouded corpse and Henry as a skeleton. Both were sons of Bess of Harwick.

A wreath sent by Queen Victoria to the funeral of Frederick Cavendish in 1882.

The font and pulpit are of 19th century design and created out of tinted marble from the Devonshire estates.

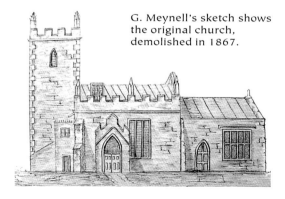

G. Meynell's sketch shows the original church, demolished in 1867.

Edlaston, St James

Mainly Decorated
This was originally a chapelry of Ashbourne and is first mentioned in the 1240 ordination charter of the vicarage of Ashbourne in which it is stated that the Dean of Lincoln, in his position as Rector of Ashbourne, should provide clergy for Kniveton, Mapleton, Thorpe, Bentley, Bradley and Edlaston when needed. Between 1291 and 1310, Edlaston became an *ecclesia* in its own right and the

Parliamentary Commissioners in 1650 said of it that: "Hedlestone is a parsonage really worth thirtye five pounds per annum. Mr Symon Waterhouse, incumbent, a frequenter of ale houses."

The chancel dates from the 14th century. Repairs and restorations were carried out c1840 and in 1870 when the east window was added. The bellcote is 1900 by E. Arden Minty.

Egginton, St Wilifrid

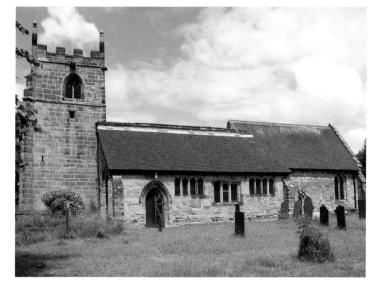

Mostly 13th century: Decorated
The Domesday Survey records that Egginton had a priest and church. There is not trace of any Norman church in the present fabric, most of which dates c1300. The tower is late Perpendicular and there are some fragments of 14th century glass in the east window. There is also a late Tudor window in the south wall. The church was restored in 1891 by Evans & Jolley.

The south aisle roof was replaced by A. Short & Partners in 2000. In 1999, the same company had added an innovative Swedish Biolet (composting toilet) to solve the problem of the church's distance from the water mains.

Elmton, St Peter

19th century

The Domesday Survey records a church and priest for Elmton and this was given to Thurgarton Priory by Ralph Deincourt.

The church was completely rebuilt in 1771-73 after it had reached a much decayed condition as pointed out in the Brief for the rebuilding of the church: ". . . the parish church of Elmton aforesaid is a very large and spacious structure consisting of Three Isles (sic) and one Cross Isle with the Steeple and Tower in the centre thereof . . . they are by length of time become very ruinous and decayed: that part of the steeple and west end of the Church are fallen down, and so much of the Church and Steeple as remained are so crooked and bulged in the foundation and walls that they cannot any longer be supported but must be wholly taken down and rebuilt." The cost of rebuilding was estimated at £1,288, and funds must have run short, as the tower was never completed.

All that remains of the original church is a slab with the inscription *"Orate pro anima Roberte Berbi"* and some gargoyles.

Elton, All Saints

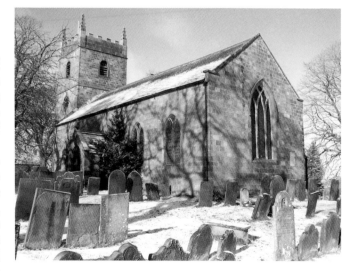

19th century

Elton was one of the chapels of Youlgreave, given along with Youlgreave church to the Abbey of Leicester during the reign of Henry II. It seems to have been known at this time as the chapel of "The Blessed Margaret of Elton".

The freeholders of the area complained to the bishop, around the end of the 17th century that "there were eighty families, poor farmers and miners, who had an antient chapel, two miles distant from the Parish church, of three aisles, three bells, and a right to bury and administer sacrament, but now by poverty . . . become destitute of Divine Service" and requested permission to mine a vein of lead ore found in the churchyard, the proceeds going to chapel funds.

In 1805, a Brief was requested for the demolition and rebuilding of the chapel as it was "a very antient structure, greatly decayed". This, however, failed to raise the needed sums and it was not until 1812 that the rebuilding was carried out.

At the time of a later restoration of the church, when the flat roofs were replaced by the present pitched ones, attempts were made to recover the original font, which had been taken to Youlgreave in 1838. Their request was to no avail and in the end they had to be content with an exact copy.

Elvaston, St Bartholomew

Mainly Decorated

There was a church and priest at Elvaston at the time of the Domesday Survey, but there is no longer any trace of the original building. The church had been given to Shelford Priory in Nottinghamshire, but was granted in 1539 to Michael Stanhope.

The chancel is c1200, but the rest of the church was completed at the expense of Lord Mountjoy of Elvaston in 1474 according to the instructions left in his will. There was an extensive restoration in 1847, in which the tower was gutted and two of the bells recast.

The chancel was restored and extended in 1904-5 by G. F. Bodley. The north chancel glass is probably by Burlison & Grylls.

J.C. Cox

Etwall, St Helen

Mainly Decorated

There was a priest and church at Etwall at the time of the Domesday Survey and the church was given to Welbeck Abbey in the second half of the 12th century.

The outside of the church presents a late Perpendicular appearance with late 17th (possibly 18th) century gothic windows. Inside, however, can be found a 12th century north arcade and a 13th century stone lectern built into the north chancel wall. The church contains the tomb of Sir John Port (d.1541), the founder of the almshouses known as Etwall Hospital and of Repton School. It was

restored in 1881 by F.J. Robinson. The 1895 east window is by Burlison & Grylls.

This is one of the churches that was damaged by the great storm of June 1545 (see Appendix).

Eyam, St Lawrence

Various

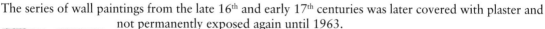

No church is mentioned here in the Domesday Survey, but the c.9th century Anglo Saxon cross in the churchyard indicates that there may have been a Saxon church on this location. Neither is there any evidence of a Norman building here, save for the Norman font. The first documentary mention of the church is in 1291 in the Taxation Roll of Pope Nicholas IV.

The present church dates from the 13th century with later 15th century Perpendicular south arcade, clerestory, nave roof and west tower.

The series of wall paintings from the late 16th and early 17th centuries was later covered with plaster and not permanently exposed again until 1963.

The church is important for its part in the 1665-66 plague when Parson Mompesson and his predecessor Thomas Stanley put the village into quarantine, thereby preventing the outward spread of infection. Mompesson's wife was one of those who died at this time and she is buried in the churchyard.

The chancel was restored in 1868–9 by G. S. Street, the north aisle being enlarged at this time and the chancel rebuilt.

The vestry is said to have been built to provide refuge for one Joseph Hunt, rector of Eyam, who had married Ann, the daughter of the village publican in a drunken mock ceremony, which the bishop subsequently forced him to make legal. Unfortunately, Joseph Hunt was already engaged to another woman who promptly sued him for breach of promise and the ensuing legal wrangles cost him so much in money and friends that he was eventually forced to take refuge in the vestry, where he remained until his death, and was buried, as recorded in a stone in the north aisle, on 16th December 1709.

The well preserved Saxon Cross

Fairfield, St Peter

Various

A chapel seems to have been built at Fairfield between 1206 and 1255, and permission to found a chantry here was granted in 1260 by the Dean and Chapter of Lichfield who held the chapel as part of the parish of Hope. In 1650, the Parliamentary Commissioners found in favour of Fairfield being united with neighbouring hamlets and made a parish.

In 1815, a petition for a Brief to allow the rebuilding of the church was submitted, stating that: "the chapel is a very ancient structure and so greatly decayed in every part that the whole fabric is in very great danger of falling . . . and also much too small. . ." The Brief was obtained but the necessary funds were not forthcoming and the rebuilding had to wait until 1838, when the old church was demolished.

The nave and tower (designed by William Swann, the village schoolmaster) were built in 1839. The south porch is 1897 and the transepts and chancel (by Garlick & Flint) were added in 1902.

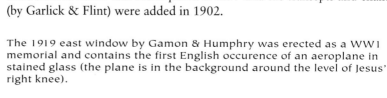

The 1919 east window by Gamon & Humphry was erected as a WW1 memorial and contains the first English occurence of an aeroplane in stained glass (the plane is in the background around the level of Jesus' right knee).

Fenny Bentley, St Edmund

Mainly Decorated

Although Fenny Bentley was one of the chapelries of Ashbourne, it became an independent *ecclesia* sometime in the 13th century, though still in the possession of the Dean and Chapter of Lincoln to whom it had been given by William Rufus along with Ashbourne. It is mentioned as such in the Taxation Roll of Pope Nicholas IV in 1291.

The nave of this church is possibly Norman although it may have been rebuilt in the 14th century and the chancel is 13th century. There is a fine 16th century screen in which can be found the motif of a fox carrying away a goose, a bitter remark on the rapacity of Lincoln.

The east window is by Norman Shaw 1877. The chancel also contains the shrouded effigies of Thomas Beresford (d.1473) and his wife Elizabeth – with his shrouded children around the sides of the tomb. This is the only example of this kind of effigy in Derbyshire, apart from that at Chesterfield church.

The church was repaired and enlarged in 1847-50 with a north aisle by H.I. Stevens. The spire was added in 1864. The altar, alter cross and candlesticks are by Advent Hunstone 1939.

The unusual Derbyshire alabaster tomb of Thomas and Agnes Beresford. This is one of only two such shrouded tombs in Derbyshire, the other being at Chesterfield. Not only are the husband and wife shown bundled up in their shrouds, but their 21 children are depicted around the sides, similarly attired. It is supposed that this is due to the tomb having been made about 100 years after the death of its occupants, at which time no likeness was available for the sculptor to work from.

The aluminium ceiling in the northeast aisle, painted by Alice M. Erskine 1895.
Fenny Bentley is probably one of the very first, if not the first, building in England to make such use of sheet aluminium.
Rolled aluminium sheet production in Britain started in December 1895 at the British Aluminium Works, Milton, Stoke-on-Trent. The sheets for the church roof were installed before October 1895. It seems likely that these were pre-production proto-types possibly given to the church by A. S. Bolton of Oakamoor, a director of the Company. His connection with Fenny Bentley is not clear however (pers. comm. Lindsey Porter).

The rood screen was given by the Beresford family in thanksgiving for the end of the War of the Roses. The detail here shows the fox – the dean of Lincoln – making off with the goose – the incomes of the parish!

The hammer beam roof with its collection of angels was added during the 19th century restorations which also saw the building of the spire.

Findern, All Saints

19th century

This was another of the chapels of Mickleover, and later became an ecclesiastical parish in its own right. It was given along with Mickleover to Burton Abbey by William the Conqueror.

The original Norman chapel, of which a rather primitive tympanum survives, was replaced in 1863-4 with the present building by Stevens & Robinson. The font dates from 1662.

The Norman tympanum has wisely been brought into the church and set into the north wall where it is protected from the elements.

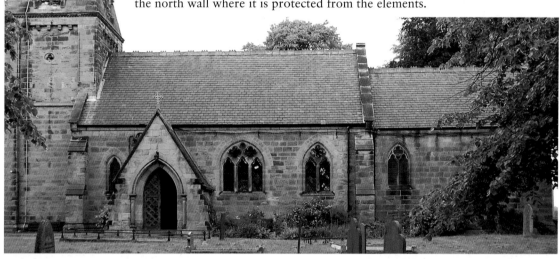

Foolow, St Hugh

19th century

Built in 1888 by reconstructing a disused smithy, which had been purchased for this purpose by a Mr Bagshawe of Sheffield and the trustee of his brother's estate. The church was opened on 17th December 1888. It is dedicated to St Hugh (1140-1200 A.D.). The font is 1890.

Foremark, St Saviour

1662: Gothic

Foremark was another of the chapels of Repton mentioned in the confirmation charters of 1271 and 1279. Of it the Parliamentary Commissioners in 1650 say: "Foremarke is a chappell heretofore a member of Repton of late united and fitt to continue soe and Milton added and Foremarke made a parish church, the chapel att Ingleby may be disused."

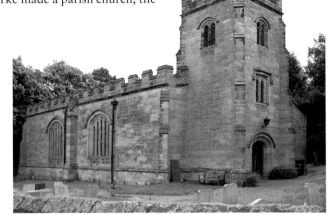

Permission was given for the demolition of the ruinous chapel at Ingleby on condition that the materials thereof be used in the construction of the bell-tower and churchyard wall of the Foremark church.

The present church was built in 1662 at the expense of Francis Burdett, and well preserved since then.

The 1710 communion rails are by Bakewell.

The box pews are original.

The font is older than the church and probably came from the older chapel here or at Ingleby.

Gamesley, Bishop Geoffrey Allen District Church

20th century
Built 1970.

Glossop, All Saints

Various

The church of Glossop was given to Basingwerk Abbey in 1157 by Henry II. Henry VIII later gave the manor and the advowson of the church to Francis Talbot, Earl of Shrewsbury.

Only one arch (east end of the north aisle) remains of the original medieval church. A Brief was applied for in 1823, stating that "the parish church is a very ancient structure, and is, by natural decay and length of time, so very ruinous, and in so great danger of falling down as to render it very unsafe for parishioners to assemble therein for the worship of Almighty God, and, notwithstanding your petitioners have expended large sums of money yearly in supporting the church, it has become necessary to take down the whole of the roof and walls and rebuild the same." Although the Brief was granted, it was not until 1831 that sufficient funds were obtained for this work. The chancel was rebuilt later, and rebuilt and extended in 1923. The original tower and spire were removed in 1853 and replaced at the expense of the Duke of Norfolk. The 1914-15 nave is by C.M. Hadfield . William Bagshawe, "The Apostle of the Peak" is said to have been vicar here.

Gosforth Valley, St Andrew's Church and School

20th century
This is a combined Anglican and URC church.

Great Longstone, St Giles

Early English style

Originally one of the chapelries of Bakewell, this church was probably already in existence when the church and chapelries of Bakewell were given to the Dean and Chapter of Lichfield by King John. It was declared by the Parliamentary Commissioners in 1650 to be "fitt to be made a parish church, and to have united to it Little Longstone, Hassop, Rowland and Monsaldale".

Cox says that the 13th century church was probably built by Griffin, son of Wenunwyn, and replaced an earlier Norman building. The church was restored in 1873 by R. Norman Shaw, a restoration which Cox much admired, saying that "Youlgreave and Longstone have been more carefully and artistically treated than any other church in the county and are models of what restoration should be". The oldest parts of the church are the 13th century lancet windows and south doorway and it is notable for its Perpendicular woodwork.

There are monuments to the Eyre family, who were originally commemorated in the east window.

Lysons records the following incident related to the church: "In the Rolls of Parliament, we find Godfrey

Rowland, who styles himself "un pauvre & simple Esquyer" praying "convenable et hasty remedy" against Sir Thomas Wendesley, John Dean vicar of Hope and others, who are stated to have come against the petitioner's house at Longesdon with force and arms, to have carried off goods and stock to the value of 200 marks, to have taken the petitioner prisoner, and carried him to the castle of the High-Peak, where he was kept in custody six days without victuals or drink; after which they are stated to have cut off his right hand, and then to have released him."

Lysons *Derbyshire*

Gresley, SS George & Mary

Decorated

A priory of Austin monks dedicated to SS Mary and Peter was founded in the first half of the 12th century by William de Gresley and dedicated to St George. The estate was sold into private hands after the dissolution of the monasteries.

In 1786, a brief was applied for to demolish and rebuild the church as it was ancient and decayed and "not fit for anybody to go into". A new church in the Italian style was proposed. The brief was granted, but sufficient funds were not forthcoming and the project was shelved.

The church was restored in 1872 with a new chancel. The tower is 15th century and there are also some earlier fragments.

Grindleford, St Helen

Various
The chancel and south side chapel by Sutton & Gregory date from 1910, but the project of building the church in this style was clearly cut short, perhaps by the Great War, leaving the nave to be added later and in a simpler style.

Hadfield, St Andrew

19th century
The Duke of Norfolk gave land for a project in 1854 to build a church school and this was used as a day school, a Sunday School and a church on Sundays. Land nearby was chosen in 1872 for the site of the church and building commenced in the November of that year. The church, by M.& H. Taylor was consecrated on the 4th July 1874 and enlarged in 1923 by C. M. Hadfield.

Handley, St Mark

19th century
The church was originally a combined school/church building, founded by the Rev J. Oldham who was the first vicar of Clay Cross on a site donated by Gladwin Turbutt of Ogston Hall. The building was opened on 18th April 1870. The roof was replaced in 2002 by A. Short & Partners.

Harpur Hill, St James

20th century
The church was built in 1910 to serve the village set up to house workers at the Harpur Quarry. Previous to that, the 1876 school had been used for worship. The land for the church was given by the Duke of Devonshire.

Hartington, St Giles

Early English and Decorated
There is no mention of the church in the Domesday Survey, but it cannot have been long after that one was built, since it is mentioned as a valuable *ecclesia* in the Taxation Roll of Pope Nicholas IV in 1291. The church was endowed upon the Minoresses, a London order of the Nuns of St Clare which was founded by Edmund, Earl of Lancaster, Leicester and Derby. The Parliamentary Survey of 1650 said that Hartington is a large parish "usually divided into four quarters" and recommended the rearranging of the parish, making the chapel of ease at Earl Sterndale into a parish church and uniting the upper quarter of the parish to Buxton. It also notes that "Mr Thomas Honeye is vicar of Hartington, reputed scandalous".

Only the north chancel wall remains from the original foundation, through the knotwork set into the clerestory window frame may date from an earlier Saxon building. The present cruciform church, very similar in plan St Mary's church at Wirksworth, dates back to the 13th century. The tower is 14th century, and it was at this time that the south transept was enlarged. This south transept was used as the Biggin chapel until that village acquired its own church in 1848.

The walls were raised in the 15th century and a clerestory added later. The porch dates from 1450. Outside, the tower and walls show a collection of

medieval and Victorian gargoyles. The church was restored in 1858 by H. Currey. Traces of old frescoes were found on the walls during this restoration, but these were not preserved.

J.C. Cox

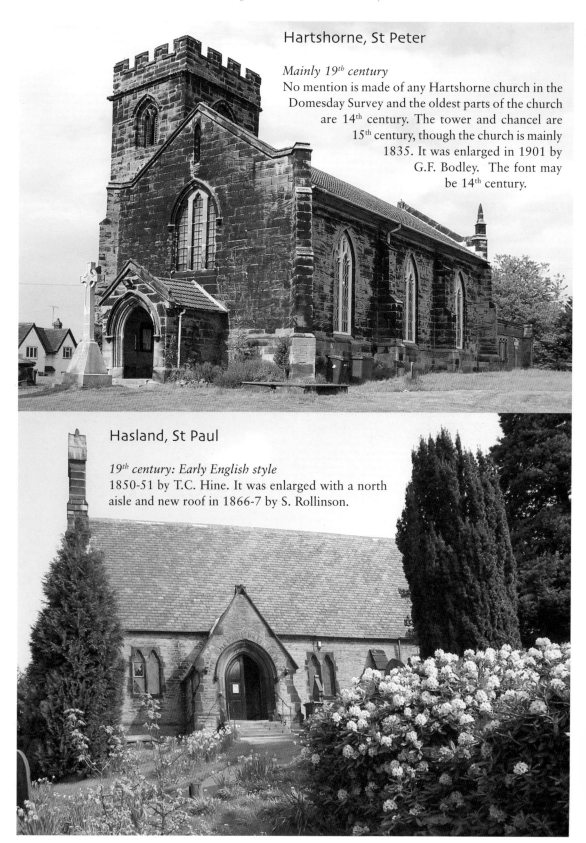

Hartshorne, St Peter

Mainly 19th century
No mention is made of any Hartshorne church in the Domesday Survey and the oldest parts of the church are 14th century. The tower and chancel are 15th century, though the church is mainly 1835. It was enlarged in 1901 by G.F. Bodley. The font may be 14th century.

Hasland, St Paul

19th century: Early English style
1850-51 by T.C. Hine. It was enlarged with a north aisle and new roof in 1866-7 by S. Rollinson.

Hathersage, St Michael and All Angels

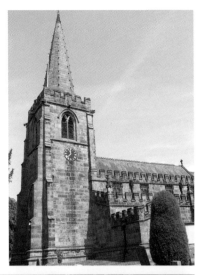

Mainly Decorated
The earliest mention of this church is towards the end of the reign of Henry I. Its advowson was among those bestowed upon the Priory of Launde. The Parliamentary Commissioners in 1650 described Hathersage (Hathersitch) as a vicarage and parish joined to Bamford, Outsetts, Bancks, Boothe and Over Padley. The church, which was supposedly built in 1381, was restored by Butterfield in 1849-52. The west tower is Perpendicular. Cox describes the church as "one of the best examples of ecclesiastical architecture that the county possesses".

The church contains 15 brasses of the Eyre family, whose name clearly inspired Charlotte Bronte who wrote *Jane Eyre* during her stay at the vicarage here in 1844.

Stained glass by Kempe was added in 1949, having been transferred from the Derwent church before the latter was submerged in the reservoir.

The graveyard is reputed to hold the grave of Little John.

J.C. Cox

Hatton, All Saints

19th century
This brick church was built in 1885–1887. There may have been an earlier chapel in this area, but no trace of one remains.

Hayfield, St Matthew

Various

This was one of the chapelries of Glossop which, along with its mother church, was owned by Basingwerk Abbey. The original chapel was said to have been built in 1386. Hayfield was declared by the Parliamentary Commissioners in 1650 as fit to be made a parish, united with neighbouring hamlets. Cox records how the chapel was put to secular use at the beginning of the 17th century, when a Grammar School was kept there for most of the century, until funds were raised for a separate building for the school. This is mentioned on a board in the church.

A brief for the restoration of the chapel was obtained in 1814 and it was completely rebuilt in 1817–18, possibly by Bradbury & Rangeley though there is some doubt about this. The tower is 1793. The church was repaired in 1953 by Taylor & Young.

Hazelwood, St John the Evangelist

19th century

Built in 1840 by H.I. Stevens and restored in 1902 (following a fire) by Naylor & Sale.

Heage, St Luke

Various

Ironically, the first mention of the church at Heage is a letter telling of its destruction in a storm on the 20th June 1545 "and from thence to Heage and there hath he [the storm] pullyed downe the chappyl and the most part of the towne . . ." (See Appendix).

The medieval church, which was a chapelry of Duffield, did not survive this storm and all that is left of it is the east window. The chancel was rebuilt in 1646-61, and a newer part was added in 1826, giving the church its T shaped layout. The Parliamentary Commissioners recommended in 1650 that Belper and Heage be united into one parish.

The church was reordered c1897 by P. H. Currey.

Heanor, St Lawrence

20th century with Perendicular tower

The manor of Heanor had a church by the time of the Domesday Survey and this was given to Burton Abbey in the 11th century. The Parliamentary Commissioners said of it that: "Heanor is a viccaridge really worth twelve pounds per annum, no chapel apperteyning. Codnor castle and Codnor Park, small things formerly distant and lying within the Constablerye are fit to be united. Mr Samuel Wright is viccar, an able man."

The original church was dedicated to St Michael, but of that building, only the 15th century tower remains, the rest having been demolished and replaced in 1868, and several times since then, the present building being the fourth of these. This was built in 1981-82 by Kenneth Murta, incorporating older elements, and was undertaken due to subsidence problems with the previous 1866 church (by Stevens & Robinson). The Perpendicular tower was retained.

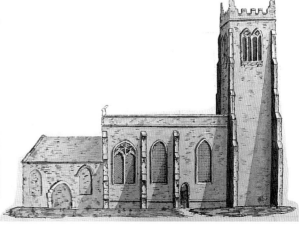

A number of fragments from the earlier buildings are kept in the present church.

Heath, All Saints

19th century: Decorated style

The parish church was given to the Abbey of Croxton in 1162 and it was probably built not long before, as no mention of it appears in the Domesday Book. The whole church, save only the porch, was demolished in 1852. The new church by H.I. Stevens was built in 1853 and restored in 1882-6 by Butterfield. The original porch still stands in the churchyard and material from the original building was used for a small chapel nearby.

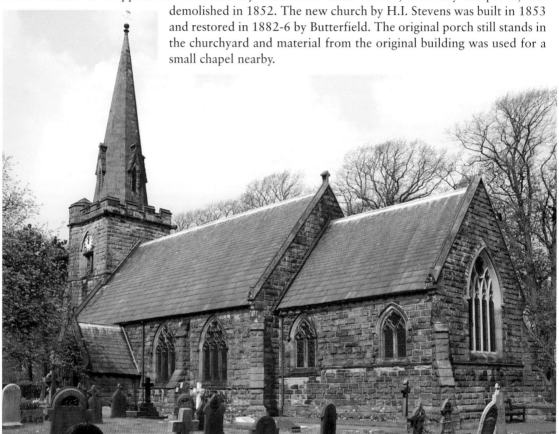

The 11th /12th century coffin slabs in the porch come from the old church nearby of which only fragments now remain.

Hognaston, St Bartholomew

Mainly 19th century

Hognaston was another of the parochial chapelries of Ashbourne. Prior to that, it would have had the less independent rank of chapel-of-ease. It was part of the gift of Ashbourne and its chapels to the Dean and Chapter of Lincoln. The Parliamentary Commissioners in 1650, mention that the curate of the time was "honest but weake".

The Norman south wall shows that the church is of an early date, probably not long after the Norman invasion, and has an extraordinary tympanum over the south door. This shows a lamb with a cross, along with a bishop and animal figures, including two fishes and the "Hognaston Hog".

The west tower is 13th century and the chancel arch is 14th century. The church underwent rebuilding by Stevens & Robinson in 1879–81 when the battlements and pinnacles were added and the nave replaced.

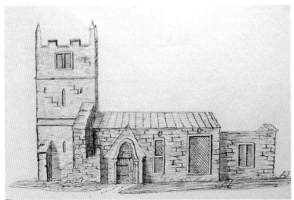

The Hognaston tympanum.

Holbrook, St Michael

18th century
This was built as a private chapel for Holbrook Hall in 1761. It became a parish church in 1835 and was enlarged in 1841. It was badly damaged by fire in 1891 and again in 1907. Following the second fire, the south aisle, chancel and porch, all by Naylor & Sale, were added.

Holloway, Christ Church

20th century:
Perpendicular Gothic style
Built by P. H. Currey in 1903 as a chapel of ease within the parish of Dethick. The central tower was added in 1911. The 1919 Arts and Crafts style east window is by Louis Davis.

Holmesdale, St Philip

20th century
This 1960s church was rebuilt and refurbished in 1994.

Holmesfield, St Swithun

19th century

This was originally a chapelry of Dronfield, but no trace remains of any earlier building. A church of St Swithun is mentioned here in 1505. A Brief of 1819 mentions that the Holmesfield chapel is "a very antient building and so ruinous it must be wholly taken down and rebuilt." The nave and tower date from 1826. The chancel by W. J. Taylor was added in 1897-8 and enlarged in 1963 by Armitage & Smith.

St Peter, Holymoorside

19th century

The 1841 chapel of St Thomas was later extended by the addition of a new nave projecting from the middle of the north wall of the church.

Hope, St Peter

Decorated and Perpendicular
It is very likely that there was a Saxon church on this site originally and the Domesday Survey notes the presence of a priest and church here. The parish later passed in to the hands of the Dean and Chapter of Lichfield Cathedral.

The aisles, clerestory and porch are 15th century and point to a general rebuild of the church during that period. The tower is early 14th century, rebuilt in 1728. The pulpit dates from 1652, and the painting of Moses and Aaron is 18th century.

The chancel was rebuilt in 1882. The east end of this was rebuilt with an enlarged east window in 1908, at which time some Kempe windows were also added.

The south side of the church has a collection of large and vividly expressive medieval gargoyles.

Horsley, St Clement

Decorated and Perpendicular
There is no mention made of a church here in the Domesday Survey, but as the church was given by Hugh de Burun to the Priory of Lenton in the reign of Stephen, it must have been built soon afterwards. In the Taxation Roll of Pope Nicholas IV, it was classified as an *ecclesia*. The Parliamentary Commissioners say that: "Horsley is a viccaridge really worth thirteene pounds and eight pence per annum and thirtye pounds from the Committee for plundered ministers paid forth of the Impropriate rectory there sequestered from the Earl of Chesterfield".

The building probably dates from the early 14th century. It was rededicated in 1450, at which time the crenellating, the clerestory and the Perpendicular windows were added. It has some good 1450 gargoyles. The church was restored in 1858-60.

Horsley Woodhouse, St Susanna

19th century
Built in 1881 – 1882 by F.J. Robinson. The east window is by Burlison & Grylls.

Hulland, Christ Church

19th and 20th century
John and Anne Bradbourne obtained permission in 1463 to build a chantry for the manor of Hough (Hulland) which they held under the Earl of Lancaster. However, there may well have been a chapel on this location at a much earlier date. Of this nothing remains – it is believed to have been demolished some time before 1750. The present building dates from 1838 by John Mason, and the original sanctuary extended by F. S. Ogden to form a chancel in 1961.

Idridgehay, St James

19th century: Decorated
Built in 1854-55 by H.I. Stevens, and consecrated in 1855.

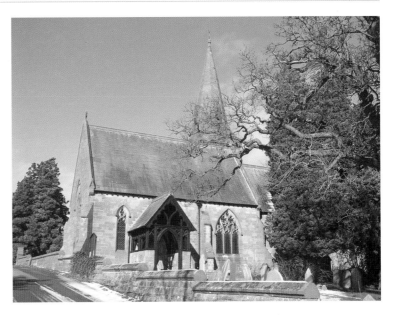

Ilkeston, Holy Trinity

19th century: Early English style
Built in 1884 by Evans & Jolley. The west part of the nave is now a church hall, while the worship area now occupies part of the chancel.

Ilkeston, St John the Evangelist

19th century: Arts and Crafts
Built in 1892-93 by Currey & Thompson in the Arts and Crafts style and enlarged in 1907-11 by P.H. Currey.

Ilkeston, St Mary the Virgin

Various
Although the church dates from c1200, there is no record of it in the Domesday Survey. It was given to Dale Abbey in 1386. The Parliamentary Commissioners said of it: "Ilkestone is a viccaridge really worth sixteene pounds per annum. Mr Fox is minister and scandalous."

Of the 1200 church, three east piers remain. The tower appears to be early 13th century but was rebuilt in 1723 and the top remodelled in 1853-5. The north chancel chapel is 14th century. In the 18th century, the church had a spire "which suffered extremely in the Hurricane of 1714" (Mr. Woolley, 1716). The tower was replaced in 1731 and the church restored extensively in 1855 by Walker & Goodacre and then enlarged by Naylor & Sale in 1909-10. The building contains glass by Burlison & Grylls (though Pevsner attributes this to P. H. Currey).

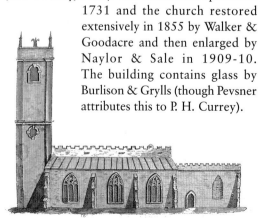

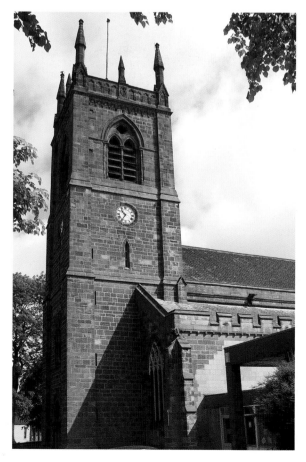

Inkersall, St Columba

20th century
1982.

Ironville, Christ Church

19th century
The church was built by the Butterley Iron Company as part of a model village and became a parish church in 1852. It is notable for the extensive use of iron in its construction, and was restored by J. R. Naylor in 1886.

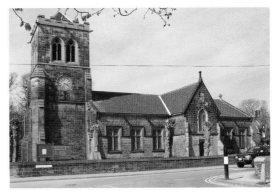

Killamarsh, St Giles

Various
The church was probably built shortly after the Domesday Survey which makes no mention of it. The earliest part (south doorway) is Norman, but the rest of the church largely dates from its late 19th century restoration, though there is an interesting 15th century stained glass window of the Virgin in the south chancel. This was recently conserved and repaired by the York Glaziers' Trust. The painted roof, dated c1450, however, is gone. There is a Saxon cross and parish stocks in the churchyard.

Lyson records the following inscription which was to be found on a tablet on the outside of the church: "To the memory of John Wright, a pauper of this parish, who died May 4th 1797, in the hundred and third year of his age. He was of middle size, temperate and cheerful, and in the trying situation of darkness, poverty, and old age, bore his infirmities with such Christian meekness as excited the benevolence of good men, and is here recorded as an instructive lesson to others. Rev C. Alderson, B.D., P.P.P, anno D⁻ni 1797". In 1895–96, the church was enlarged with a north aisle and the chancel was extended eastward by J.M. Brooks.

King Sterndale, Christ Church

19th century: Early English style
This church by I. Bonomi and J.A. Cory was consecrated by the Bishop of Lichfield on 12th July 1849. The pulpit and lectern are by Advent Hunstone. It has in the past been part of the Diocese of Lichfield, then Southwell and became part of the Diocese of Derby in 1927.

Kirk Hallam, All Saints

Mainly Decorated
Norman in origin but now mainly 14th and 15th century. Norman beakheads survive in the porch and the font is Norman. The church was repaired in 1844 and restored in 1859 by G.E. Street.

Kirk Ireton, Holy Trinity

Various

This was a chapelry of Wirksworth and thus given, along with the latter, to the Dean and Chapter of Lincoln, by Henry I. By the time of the Taxation Roll of Pope Nicholas IV in 1291, it had become an independent *ecclesia*, though Lincoln still retained the advowson. The Parliamentary Commissioners in 1650 considered the incumbent Peter Watkinson to be "able and godlye".

The church underwent extensive alterations in the 14th century and the chancel dates from this time. The tower is Perpendicular and the clerestory was added

much later, in the early 18th century. The church was restored and south aisle windows and clerestory added in 1885 by Bodley & Garner.

Unfortunately, the Norman font illustrated by Meynell no longer exists since, Cox records, "within recent years, a pagan-minded plumber lighted a fire under it to melt some lead, and, of course, split it to pieces". Previous to this, according to Meynell, it had been used to catch rainwater.

Kirk Langley, St Michael and All Angels

Early English, Decorated

There is no record of a church here in the Domesday Survey. The manor of Langley was held, at that time, by Levenot, under Ralph Fitz Hubert. When the manor was divided, one part became known as Meynell Langley, being owned by the Meynell family and the other as Kirk Langley from the existence there of the church. This original church appears to have been largely rebuilt in the early 14th century. It was later damaged in the storm of 20th June 1545: " . . . And from thence he went to Langley wch is lyke iiij myles from Darby, & there he hath pullyd downe a great p^te of the church & rowled up the leade and left it lying . . ." see Appendix. The Parliamentary Commissioners, in 1650, said of it: "Kirk Langley is a parsonage really worth three score pounds per annum. Mr Francis Alsop Incumbent able preacher and of godly conversation."

A day school was held in the church until 1750. A vestry was added (at the expense of Godfrey Meynell) in 1824 and the church was renewed in 1839. It was restored again in 1885 by Bodley & Garner, who also added the south aisle windows and clerestory. The east window is by Burlison & Grylls.

Kniveton, St Michael and All Angels

Various

Kniveton was originally a chapelry of Ashbourne and given along with the mother church to the Dean and Chapter of Lincoln by William Rufus. It became an independent *ecclesia* in the 13th century. The original dedication seems to have been to John the Baptist, but later came to be St Michael and All Angels.

Kniveton appears in the Domesday Book as the Manor of Cheniveton, but no church is mentioned. However, the oldest parts of the present church date from the 12th century. The nave is Norman, as is the porch with a bear in the keystone of the south door. The chancel is 14th/15th century and the tower and spire 13th century. Fragments of the 14th and 15th century glass may be seen in the south window of the sanctuary, though the glass in the nave is from 1888 onwards. The church was restored in 1870.

Langley Mill, St Andrew

20th century: Arts and Crafts

Built in 1911-3 by J.S. Brocklesby in Derbyshire stone at a cost of £8,000. The church was consecrated by the bishop of Southwell on 8th October 1912 and became part of the diocese of Derby in 1926. In 1987 it became a joint Anglican/Methodist church.

Linton & Castle Gresley, Christ Church

19th century
1881.

Little Eaton, St Paul

19th century: Norman style
Originally a chapel of St Alkmund's church, the Parliamentary Commissioners of 1650 declared Little Eaton "fitt to be united to Birdsall". By 1760, the chapel had descended into a "ruinous condition" and came to be used as a blacksmith's shop. In 1791, this ruin was demolished and replaced with a new building which was enlarged in 1837 and 1851. It then underwent a massive modernisation, in the Norman style,

in 1851 under H.I. Stevens, at which time the tower was added. It was enlarged in 1869 by Giles & Brookhouse.

Littleover, St Peter

Mainly 19th century
This was originally a chapelry of Mickleover, but later became an ecclesiastical parish. The building is Norman, but has been much restored, leaving only the Norman doorway which is now the door to the belfry. The north aisle (along with a new vestry and porch) was added in 1856 by H.I. Stevens and the south aisle by Naylor & Sale in 1908. The west end was enlarged by Sebastian Comper in 1959-61.

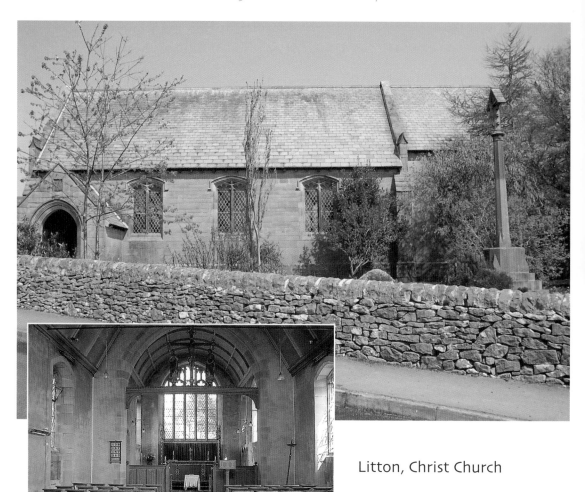

Litton, Christ Church

20th century: Traditional style
Built in 1926-7 by W.H.R Blacking.

Long Eaton,
St John the Evangelist

20th century
Built in 1922 by Charles Nicholson. The interior was later modernised by Montague Associates. A southwest tower was planned but was never built

Long Eaton, St Laurence

Decorated
Originally a chapel of Sawley, it was made a parochial chapelry in 1838 and then became a vicarage in 1864. The Norman structure was rebuilt in the 14th century, and the Norman south doorway survives. The building was enlarged in 1868 by G.E. Street at which time the north aisle, nave and chancel were added. The tower is 15th century.

Long Lane, Christ Church

19th century: Gothic style
The church, by Hine & Evans, was built in 1859. The tower and vestry were added in 1874.

Longford, St Chad

Various: Mainly Early English

The earliest mention of the church at Longford appears in 1145 when the church was given to Gresley Priory. Although neither the church nor the manor of Longford is mentioned in the Domesday Survey, the Norman origins of the church can be seen in some of the arcading and pillars as well as the Norman font, but the present structure is mainly 14th and 15th century. There are a number of monuments to members of the Longford family who were Lords of the Manor here until the 16th century, and their successors, the Cokes.

The Parliamentary Commissioners describe it as "a parsonage and a viccaridge . . . noe chapel apperteyning."

The church was repaired in 1843-44 by H.I. Stevens.

Longford family effigies. These were previously on the floor of the south aisle but in 1984 they were cleaned and conserved by Harrison Hill Ltd and placed on new tomb chests.

Loscoe, St Luke

20th century
The origins of this church lie in the small mission church built by the Butterley Company and consecrated on 8th March 1924.

In 1927, Loscoe was constituted an ecclesiastical parish and the foundation stone of the present building by Bernard Widdows was laid in 1936. The church was consecrated in 1937.

Loundsley Green, Church of the Ascension

20th century
1964.

Lullington, All Saints

Early English/Decorated
No church is mentioned at Lullington in the Domesday Survey, although it did have a priest. According to Cox, this probably indicates that the priest's Saxon church had been destroyed following the Norman Conquest. In any case, a church was soon built there again and the advowson given to Gresley Priory.

Only the tower and spire survive from the old church, though the spire was rebuilt in 1776. The church itself was rebuilt in 1778-1799 and again in 1861, after which time the south aisle and chancel by J.W. Hugall were added.

The registers, which begin in 1560, record that in 1642 "Philip Greensmith a soldier was executed upon a Tree at the green of Coton for deserting his colours, March 31st. The Tree dyed by degrees."

Mackworth, St Francis

20th century
1953-4 by Milburn & Partners. It was originally built as an east facing church but was later turned to face west instead.

Mackworth, All Saints

Decorated/Perpendicular
The chartulary of Darley Abbey mentions a church at Mackworth, and there was certainly one here by 1200, though the church mentioned in this connexion in the Domesday Survey was probably the one at Markeaton. The Parliamentary Commissioners said of it : "Mackworth is a parsonage and viccaridge impropriate. Francis Mundy Esq is Impropriator receives the profits w[ch] are really worth two hundred and fiftye pounds per annum and procures the cure supplied as he can agree, destitute at present."

Pevsner says that the west tower of this church is "supposed to have defensive purposes" as the door into the nave can be barred and the tower has no door to the outside, as well as having only small windows on the lower levels. There are also cross-bow loop holes on the west and north of the tower, very rare on churches.

Much of the building is 13th and 14th century, but it was enthusiastically decorated and restored in 1851 with details such as the elaborate alabaster decorations and the 1903 lectern with vine and grapes.

There is a room over the porch, which until 1851 had a fireplace and chimney, perhaps for the accommodation of a chaplain or sacristan. This had squints (small holes in a wall) allowing the inhabitant to keep watch over the side altars.

J. C. Cox

Mapperley, Holy Trinity

20th century
The original Early English style 1851 church by T.D. Barry was replaced in 1966, due to subsidence caused by local mining. The modern building incorporates some elements of the older, such as the stained glass.

Mappleton, St Mary

18th century: Tuscan
Although the village is mentioned in the Domesday Book, the church itself is not. It would have been one of the chapelries of Ashbourne, given to Lincoln, but it is mentioned in the Taxation Roll of Pope Nicholas IV as an *ecclesia* independent from Ashbourne. The first historical reference to the church occurs during the reign of Edward I and a survey in 1547 records that it possessed 13 bells (probably handbells!).

The church was declared to be "fit to be disused" in 1650, but it was not until much later that the replacement was carried out, by which time it had become extremely dilapidated. A of 1887 dates the new church to 1710, but a date around 1752 is probably more accurate. The design, by James Gibbs, is 18th century and simple with a distinctive tower surmounted by octagonal dome and domed lantern. The porch was originally part of the south wall and more ornate.

Marlpool, All Saints

20th century
This red brick church was built in 1908 by Naylor and Sale and rebuilt in 1950 following a fire.

Marston Montgomery, St Giles

Norman with 19th century additions
The manor of Marston Montgomery is not mentioned in the Domesday Survey. However, it appears to have been included in the manor of Cubley and the church actually at Marston may have been the one recorded in the Survey as being the Cubley church, as parts of the Marston church are older than the one at Cubley. Once the larger church at Cubley had been built, the Marston church became its chapel, as recorded in the Parliamentary Commissioners in 1650: "Marston Montgomery is a chappell apperteyning (to Cubley)." From 1660, it became a parochial chapelry.

The nave and chancel are Norman with a 13th century north aisle. The south doorway is Norman and it is possible that the chancel arch is Saxon. The church was much altered in 1824 – the Meynell drawing, made in 1817, shows it having flat roofs at different levels. The church was enlarged with a new north aisle by St Aubyn (who also added the bellcote) in 1878.

The east window is by Burlison & Grylls.

Marston on Dove, St Mary

Decorated

The Domesday Survey shows Marston on Dove as having a church and a priest. Even at this point, the church was held by the Priory of Tutbury, under Henry de Ferrers.

Cox thinks that the true dedication of the church is to St John and later plans show a dedication to St John the Divine.

The church has a c1200 chancel with a c1350 south aisle and west tower. There are traces of the Norman original in the fabric of the church. The clerestory was added in the 15th century. The building was much altered in 1816, and the original stone porch replaced with one of brick. Battlements and steeple appear to have been added in 1755. The building was reroofed in 2003 by A. Short & Partners.

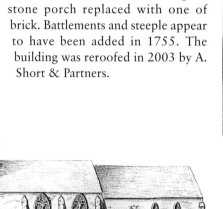

The church possesses the oldest bell in Derbyshire as well as a very old font which appears to date back to the church mentioned in the Domesday Survey.

Matlock Bank, All Saints

19th century

The choir, to a design by T.H. and F. Healey, was completed in 1884, along with part of the nave. However, lack of funds led to the church being finished in a truncated and hasty manner. The entrance hall, baptistery and gallery were designed by C. H. Porter and added in 1958.

The glass at the east end is by Morris & Co to a design by Burne-Jones and the 1935 oak parclose screens around the choir stalls are by Advent Hunstone.

Matlock Bath, Holy Trinity

19th century: Decorated style
The church was built by Weightman & Hadfield at a cost of £2,250 and consecrated on the 5th October 1842. The south aisle was added and the chancel extended in 1874 by T.E. Streatfield. It was later refurbished to include the addition of a baptistry designed for baptism by immersion, though this is no longer in use and has been floored over.

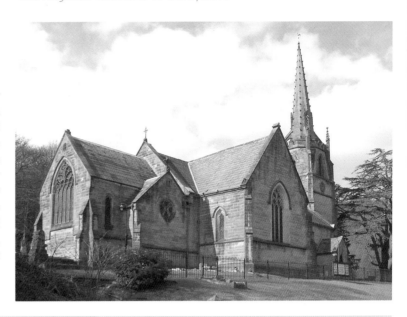

Matlock, St Giles

Various
The Domesday Survey makes no mention of a church at Matlock, but it must have been built soon after, probably in the early 12th century. There was some rebuilding in 1760, when the south aisle wall was rebuilt. There was a clerestory level, which was removed at some point and some of the stone piers were replaced by cast iron columns. There was some more rebuilding of the north aisle in 1873 by Richard Arkwright who had purchased the manor of Willersley (which had rights over this aisle) the year before.

The chancel was rebuilt in 1859 and the nave was taken down in 1871 and rebuilt by B. Wilson of Derby. The Perpendicular tower remains and the church possesses a large Norman font. A south chapel by P. H. Currey was added in 1898.

The original porch has been rebuilt into the wall to the right of the present south porch.

Melbourne, SS Michael & Mary

Norman

The Domesday Survey mentions that the manor of Melbourne was possessed of a church and a priest. The revenues of this church were endowed upon the bishopric of Carlisle.

The church probably originated prior to 1100. The exterior of this cruciform building is incomplete – the two west towers were either unfinished or suffered subsequent damage. Inside, the great arcades and impressive clerestory give the church one of the most important Norman interiors in the country.

The tower over the crossing was built up higher in the 17th century and a belfry was added at this time. A restoration was carried out in 1859-62 under Sir Gilbert Scott, and the two west towers were given slated roofs at this time. The chancel windows are 1867 and 1869 by J. Hardman.

J. C. Cox

Stone carvings can be found inside, in the capitals of the crossing arches, and outside, with figures of fertility symbols and devils harking back to the country's pre Christian past.

Mellor, St Thomas

Early English

There may have been a chapel here in the early part of the 12th century, but there is no definite record of this. The chapelry would have been part of the Glossop group appropriated by Basingwerk Abbey.

The only original part of this chapel which survives is the tower, though most of this appears to be from the 15th century. There is also some older fabric in the church.

It was declared by the Parliamentary Commissioners in 1650 to be a chapelry of Glossop "fitt to be made a parish church with hamlets of Whitell, Hamell, part of Thornsett, Ludworth and Chisworth."

A Brief for the Church's rebuilding was petitioned for in 1815, but sufficient funds were not raised and it took a further two Briefs until repairs could be made in 1824 – at which time Archdeacon Butler ordered that the chancel should be immediately taken down and rebuilt.

The small window is by William Whittam on the theme of Christ as the light of the world, and before it stands a Madonna commissioned by Robin Phillip in memory of his wife Ethelda. It is by Vincent Butler of Edinburgh and was dedicated in 1993.

The interesting Norman font may be 11th century or maybe even earlier, from the Danish appearance of the mounted figures riding around it.

The 13th century pulpit was carved in one piece from the trunk of an oak tree and may be the oldest of its kind anywhere.

Mickleover, All Saints

19th century: Early English style
Although William the Conqueror gave the town of Mickleover, with its church, to Burton Abbey, no mention is made in the Domesday Survey of there being a church here. The Taxation Rolls of Pope Nicholas IV speak of it as an *ecclesia* and of it the Parliamentary Commissioners said: "Mickleworth is a viccaridge having two chapels apperteyning, really worth one hundred pounds per annum (vizt) Mickleover itself fyfte pounds, Littleover twentye fowre pounds and Finderne six and twentye pounds. Mr William Harcott is viccar, a man insufficient and scandalous".

   Although the present church has 14th century origins with stonework in the tower dating from that time, the main body of the church dates from the rebuilding and enlargement by H.I. Stevens in 1858-9, possibly following a fire. The vestry and north aisle chapel are 1965-7 by G.I. Larkin and the east window is by C. Gibbs.

Mickleover, St John

20th century
Modern church, built in 1970s to replace a defective post war building.

Middleton by Wirksworth, Holy Trinity

19th century: Perpendicular style
Built in 1838 by T. Newton. There are schoolrooms underneath main building. The church was enlarged in 1878-82 by F.J. Robinson. The west porch dates from 1925 and is by Naylor, Sale & Woore as are the vestries.

Middleton by Youlgreave, St Michael and All Angels

19th century: Early English style
This would seem to have been one of the chapels of Youlgreave at the time when it was given to the Abbey of Leicester during the reign of Henry II. Of the ancient chapel nothing remains, although Cox mentions that "The museum of the late Mr Bateman contains – 'A crowned female corbel head of good work, from Middleton' . . . and a small cross in the form of a quatrefoil, with a rose in the centre, cut from a thick piece of sandstone, which was found in a wall at Middleton, in 1828" along with some "architectural fragments" which may have been part of the original chapel.

Permission was granted in 1864 for the building of a mission church which later became the parish church.

Milford, Holy Trinity

19th century: Early English style
The surrounding village would have originally been called Muleford – being located at the crossing point for the packhorse route from Wirksworth.

The church, by W.B. Moffatt, was opened in July 1848, having been built on land given by the Strutt family.

Miller's Dale, St Anne

19th century: Perpendicular style
Built in 1879, probably H.Cockbain.
The church contains carvings by Advent
Hunstone and embroidery by Morris &
Co.

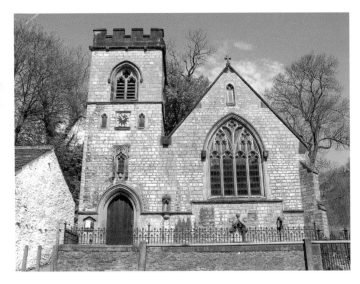

Monyash, St Leonard

Various
This was founded as a chantry chapel
c.1200 by Robert de Salocia and
Matthew de Eston. It was a chapel of
the mother church at Bakewell and was
included in the gift of this church and
its associated chapels to the Dean and
Chapter of Lichfield. Monyash was
declared by the Parliamentary
Commissioners in 1650 to be fit to be
made a parish.

Some Norman pieces remain, such as
the sedilia and piscina, though much of
the rest is 13th and 14th century and the
octagonal font is 15th century. The north
and south transepts were built in the
14th century but had disappeared by the 19th century. Cox urged that a careful search
for their foundations be made and sure enough, both were rebuilt during Butterfield's
restoration of the building in 1887. During this restoration the encaustic floor tiles
in the chancel were added, along with the roof trusses and pews.

The chancel and tower were also rebuilt at this time, as was the tower.

The absence of the south transept can
be seen from Meynell's sketch

Morley, St Matthew

Various

Morley is first mentioned by Wulfric Spott in the endowment charter of Burton Abbey in 1002. He left part of the manor to the Abbey. The church itself is not mentioned in the Domesday Survey, but this was probably an oversight, as it is likely that there was a church here at this time. It was given to Chester Abbey in 1186-1194. The Parliamentary Commissioners (Parliamentary Survey of Livings 1650) said of it: "Morley is a parsonage . . . and hath a chappell att Smawley apperteyning a myle distant. Mr John Harpur Incumbent a man able and honest."

The church is very important for its medieval stained glass and well documented architectural history. The building is Norman with later additions, such as the 14th century stained glass from Dale Abbey in the northeast chapel and the medieval floor tiles and south porch.

The south arcade is Norman, the north is 13th century and the chancel seems to be early 14th century. The chancel chapel was added in 1380 by Ralph de Stathum who died in 1380. The west tower was given by his widow who died in 1403 and the south chapel by John Stathum who died in 1453.

The clerestory was added in the 15th century. There are a very large number of interesting medieval monuments, some of very high quality.

The church was extensively repaired in 1800, having suffered from a custom recorded by a Mr Fox in c1829: ". . . it was the custom of the friends and visitors at the village, at times of hospitality, such as Christmas and the Wakes to show their regard for the church and its interesting objects, but pulling a bit of stained glass out of the windows to take home as a relic or as an object of amusement for children."

Another thorough restoration was carried out c1850 under the direction of G. G. Place.

The St Ursula in the window is medieval, but the rest of the glass is 19th century.

This collection of 14th century stained glass was brought to the church from Dale Abbey at the time of the Dissolution of the Monasteries. It underwent some repair and additions in 1847 by W. Warrington.

The 1897 Bateman Mausoleum by G. F. Bodley stands in the churchyard as does a 1762 sundial.

Medieval floor tiles in the north chapel date back to c1370. These were gathered together from various parts of the church and laid in their present location during the 1850s restoration. Three of the four incised slabs to the Sacheverell children can be seen here, all dating from the early to mid-17th century.

Morton, Holy Cross

Mainly 19th century: Decorated style
Morton is mentioned in the Domesday book as being owned by Walter Deincourt and as having a church and a priest. It has a 13th century north arcade and 15th century tower. The rest is by T.C. Hine in 1850 and G.M.R. Turbutt who enlarged it in 1912-13. The church possesses a Saxon font.

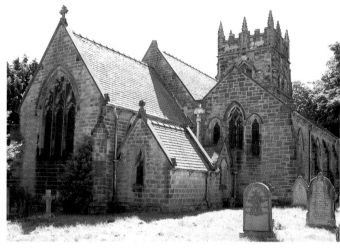

An unusual double gargoyle, high in the west tower.

Mugginton, All Saints

Various
There was a church and priest at Mugginton at the time of the Domesday Survey. The tower is Norman, with later alterations and there are a few other Norman remnants in the body of the church. It contains extensive 13th and 14th century additions and a Perpendicular chancel. The south aisle was lengthened towards the east in the mid 15th century. The church was renovated in 1845.

Halter Devil Chapel

18th century

Closely associated with Mugginton Church, this chapel was founded by Francis Brown in 1723. It supposedly got its name from a story (there are many variations on this tale) that this Brown, being drunk, insisted one stormy night, on riding to Derby. When his wife tried to persuade him not to, he swore that he would go even if he had to halter the Devil himself. When he went out to catch his horse, he found the beast had grown horns, and so fainted in terror. When he recovered, he built the chapel as a token of his

The tiny interior of Halter Devil Chapel

repentance and new found sobriety. Cox remarks prosaically that the drunken Brown, had probably tried to halter a cow which, objecting to such a proceeding, had knocked him senseless with a well aimed kick. In 1731, this chapel was annexed to Mugginton, though in the early 19th century, the chapel was apparently used as a dairy during the week. The house against which the chapel was built, once carried the following verse:

"Francis Brown in his old age
Did build him here a hermitage
Who being old and full of evil
Once on a time haltered the Devil"

Netherseal, St Peter

Mostly 19th century

The north tower is Perpendicular and the church has some 13th century features. Most of the church, however, is by Blomfield and dates from 1877.

New Houghton, Christ Church

19th century
1897.

New Mills, St George

19th century: Early English style
Built in 1830 by R. D. Chantrell with tower and spire in Gothic style. The chancel, by Preston & Vaugham, was added in 1898 when the interior was recorded. The original galleries remain as does the 1845 organ case.

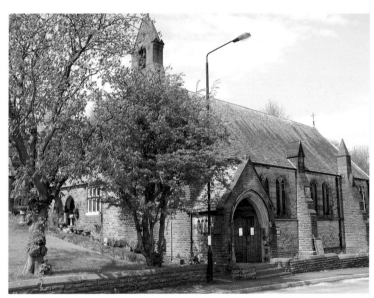

New Mills, St James the Less

19th century
Built in 1878–80 by W. Swinfen Barber. The interior survives as decorated by Powell with painted roof and wall murals. There is also a stained glass window of the Crucifixion by Kempe.

The church was intended as a chapel of ease for St George's above.

New Whittington, St Barnabas

19th century
The church was built in 1884 as a mission church and became a parish in its own right in 1927.

Newbold, St John the Evangelist

19th century

The Newbold Chapel on this site would have been, at one time, the mother church of Chesterfield. This chapel, in turn, stood on the site of an earlier Norman building, parts of which were incorporated into the chapel. However it was badly damaged during the reign of William III and was subsequently used as a cowshed and barn until replaced with the new church by Flockton & Son in 1857. The wide north and south aisles by W.H.R. Blacking were added in 1957.

Newhall, St John

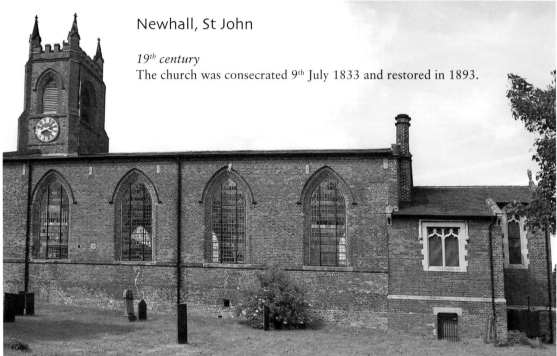

19th century

The church was consecrated 9th July 1833 and restored in 1893.

Newton Solney, St Mary the Virgin

Various

This was another of the chapels of Repton as mentioned in the confirmation charters of the latter in 1271 and 1279. Newton Solney was one of the estates of Henry de Ferrers.

The building is 14th century with some Norman remnants, such as the doorway in the north wall of the tower. The roof was renewed in the 17th century and the church was rebuilt in 1880 by F. J. Robinson.

Norbury, SS Mary and Barlok

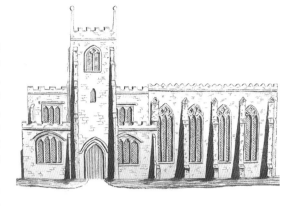

Decorated Gothic

The Domesday Survery records a church and priest for Norbury. This church was already in the possession of Tutbury Priory, to whom it had been given by Henry de Ferrers. The church and its tithes later passed into the hands of William Fitzherbert in fee-farm, and the advowson remained with the Fitzherberts until 1538, when it was seized by the Crown on account of the Catholicism of the Fitzherbert family.

The Parliamentary Commissioners said of the church in 1650: "Norburye is a parsonage and hathe a parochiall Chappell fayre and large apperteyning thereunto att Snelstone (. . .) There is butt one house at Norbury where the parish Church is and Snelstone is a myle distant and a large towne and fitt to be made the parish church and Norbury disused."

Fortunately, this resolution was never put into effect, since this church – probably built between 1349 and 1395 by Henry Kniveton – is one of the most important churches of Derbyshire, in particular for the magnificent c1305 stained glass in the chancel. The nave, south tower and chapel (by the tower) were built by Nicholas Fitzherbert who died in 1473 and it is either he or his son Ralph who also gave the church its north aisle. The church was renovated in 1842.

St Barlok, to whom the church is dedicated, was an Irish bishop and abbot. He appears in the window of the south chapel.

The windows date from c1305 and as part of the renovations by A. Short & Partners are being restored and releaded by Holywell Glass.

The south transept window was restored by the York Glaziers' Trust.

The well-preserved Saxon cross shaft, now kept inside the church.

The missing stained glass to the lower left dates from an incident in 1984 when a burglar was locked in the church to await the police and made his escape by hurling a chair through the window.

Normanton-by-Derby, St Giles

19th century

The earliest mention of a church here is in 1288, in documents concerning a dispute between the abbot of Darley Abbey and the parishioners over repairs and maintenance of the building. However, the church was much older, possibly pre-Norman.

The Parliamentary Commissioners said of it: "Normanton is another chappell apperteyning to Peters the profits thereof is accompted for in the first mentioned fortye pounds and both Osmaston and Normanton lye neare to Peters are fitt to continue and both chappells disused."

The old church was demolished in 1861 and replaced with the present building by Giles & Brookhouse. Of the original church, only the Norman tympanum and tower survive.

The south aisle was extended westwards by Naylor & Sale in 1893. Naylor & Sale also added a new chancel, south arcade and south aisle in 1900-01.

North Wingfield, St Lawrence

Various

The parish is mentioned in the 1086 Domesday Survey as having a church and priest, but there are no remains of this, apart, possibly from the font. The church was given to the Priory of Thurgarton by Ralph Deincourt.

The present church is 15th century and has a 14th century chancel although there is a late Norman (probably middle of 12th century) window in the north transept. This window was restored in 1872, probably by S. Rollinson, at which time some early 12th century incised slabs were found during the demolition of the north wall for the restoration of the north aisle. The church was more widely restored in 1879 by R.H. Carpenter.

The 80ft tower is 15th century and the east window dates from 1320. The screen, in the style of a 15th century rood loft is by Sir Thomas Jackson in 1917.

There is an ancient font, which was used at one point as a washbasin by local schoolboys on their way to dinner. This font may well have been part of the original church.

The church was reordered in 1998–1999 by A. Short & Partners.

Oakwood,
The Church on Oakwood

20th century
1993.

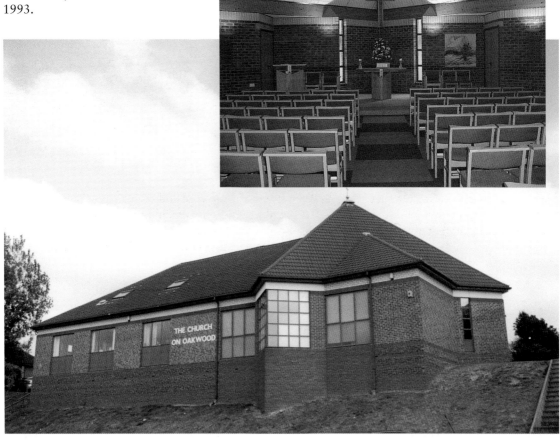

Ockbrook, All Saints

Various
Until after the Reformation, Ockbrook was a chapelry of Elvaston and its tithes were appropriated to the Shelford monastery. It had become a vicarage in its own right by 1620. The west tower is 12th century but the chancel was rebuilt for Thomas Pares in 1803. The font is Norman and the 16th century glass in the east window was brought from Wigston's Hospital in Leicester by Thomas Pares. The church was repaired and enlarged in 1814–1815 and again in 1835 by John Mason.

Old Brampton, SS Peter and Paul

Various

There was a chapel on this site as far back as 1100, but the church was rebuilt and consecrated in 1253 by Brendon, Bishop of Ardfert (now part of the diocese of Limerick, Ireland). Some Norman traces do remain, such as the south doorway.

A Brief from 1823 stated that "The church of our parish . . . is an ancient structure, is greatly dilapidated, arising from damps and age, and the interior parts, having been injudiciously arranged in the original planning of them, will not accommodate the larger part of a now much increased population." The subsequent alterations by J. Hobson cost £669 and involved reordering and opening up the interior by removing heavy galleries and adding windows. The church was altered again in 1868 by S. Rollinson.

Cox records a bizarre custom whereby the corpse of the first person in Brampton or its related hamlets to die after New Year's Day was to be taken to Chesterfield for burial, the vicar of Chesterfield receiving "all the fees and mortuary oblations" for this individual. This was continued until around 1828 when the inhabitants of Brampton mounted a successful legal challenge. At the time of Cox's writing (1875), the corpse was no longer transferred to Chesterfield, but the sum of two shillings was paid to the vicar of Chesterfield for the first to die in the New Year.

Meynell's sketch shows the Peter and Paul figures still on the outside of the church.

Stone slab to Matilda le Caus, d.1224.

St Peter. The figures of Peter and Paul are c1300 and were originally on the outside of the church, on the south wall. They were conserved by Harrison Hill Ltd in 1988, brought inside the church and set into the west wall of the nave.

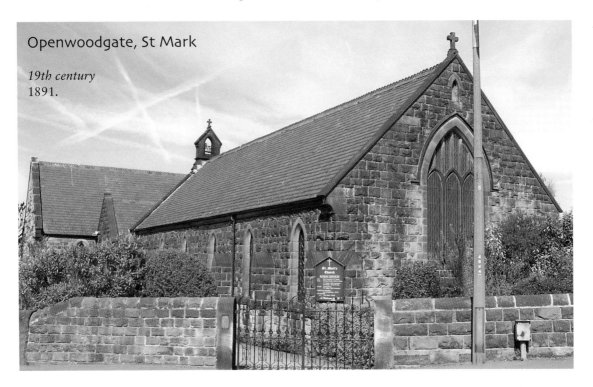

Openwoodgate, St Mark

19th century
1891.

Osmaston, St Martin

19th century: Medieval Gothic style
There is no mention of a church here in the Domesday Survey, though a stone in the old church was engraved with the date *A.D. cccccc* which was thus claimed to be the date of the original foundation. However, such an early date is unlikely, and there is no other record of a church here until the 14th century.

Osmaston was a parochial chapelry of Brailsford until it became an independent parish in the 19th century. The Parliamentary Commissioners had already recommended this in 1650: "Osmaston wee think fit to be made a parish of itselfe with the Addison of some adjacent places." The Commission also remarked that the curate was "a man insufficient and scandalous".

The original chapel (which is said to have been built of wickerwork) was demolished around 1843 and replaced at a cost of £8,000. Paid for by Francis Wright, and designed by H. I. Stevens, this is the first church in Derbyshire built in the Medieval Gothic style. It was considered radical for its time and place, with its high pitched roofs, structural buttresses and array of stone tracery and reflects H.I. Stevens' enthusiastic conversion to the principles of the Oxford Movement.

The church was consecrated on the 25th June 1845.

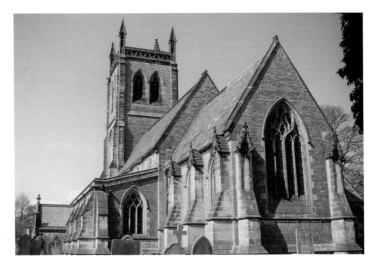

Over Haddon, St Anne

19th century: Gothic style
Built in 1880 by H. Cockbain. The parish was at one time noted for being the birthplace and home of a famous "fasting damsel" who was said to have started her fast on 22nd December 1667 at the age of 18 and by 1669, according to a number of pamphlets published about her, was still alive and in good health, although there was no moisture in her nose and mouth, she was extraordinarily thin and suffered from severe insomnia. She was watched round the clock on two occasions by 40 to 50 women – the second time on the instigation of the Earl of Devonshire. It appears from the parish registers that she died 15 years later, but there is no record of whether her fast was continued, given up or found to be a hoax. She inspired the fraudulent imitator Ann Moor of Tutbury who finally gave up her own fast and confessed.

The 1977 sundial is in memory of Janet Wadsworth.

Overseal, St Matthew

19th century
Built in 1840-1 by Thomas Johnson.

Palterton, St Luke

19th/20th century
Mission Room.

Parwich, St Peter

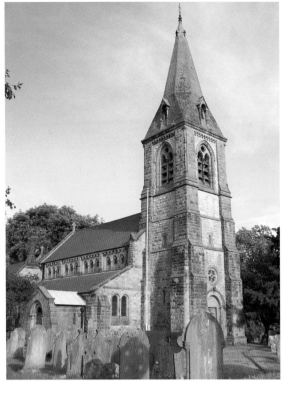

19th century: Late Norman/Early English style
Originally a chapelry of Ashbourne, the earliest mention of the church itself is in 1240 in the Endowment Charter of the Vicarage of Ashbourne, in which the vicar of Ashbourne is given the duty of providing a chaplain for Parwich. The Parliamentary Commissioners recommended in 1650, that it be made into a parish church and Alsop-en-le-Dale united to it.

The original Norman building was demolished in 1872 and replaced in 1873 with a larger structure by Stevens & Robinson, at the expense of T.W. Evans of Allestree Hall. Not all the parishioners appreciated the change:

"Where is now the low, ivy covered square tower, through which one entered and saw the sexton toll the bell? Where is the sculptured sword, thought to be crusaders? Where the pulpit for the Parson with the desk under it for the clerk? Where the choir with its diverse instruments of music in the gallery? Where the square pews that belonged to several farms and gave a special and personal interest to the occupants? All gone! All swept away to satisfy the ritualistic fancies of a sacerdotal parson. Thus is England being spoiled of its glory" (Notes by Joseph Thompson of Parwich 1833-1909).

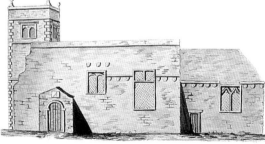

Sketch by Meynell of the original church. A south gallery with an external staircase was added in 1815, but does not appear here.

The tympanum over the south door was, at the time of the demolition of the Norman church, covered with thick plaster whitewash. During the building of the new church, this plaster was cleaned away and its extraordinary figures revealed: a lamb with a cross and a stag, with a serpent or dragon below. Above the lamb is a bird and above the stag, a pig and a lion. It was then incorporated into the new building over the west door in which position it is now deteriorating rapidly due to exposure to the elements.

Peak Dale, Holy Trinity

19th century
1886.

Peak Forest, Charles, King and Martyr

19th century

The present church is 1876–7 by H. Cockbain, built on the site of a 1657 chapel which was, Cox reports, built at the expense of the Countess of Devonshire. However, he points out that although she was a fervent monarchist, she would hardly "have been daring enough to dedicate a chapel to Charles, King and Martyr in 1657". It is likely, therefore, that the chapel was completed and dedicated after the Restoration. It was an 'extra-parochial' and extra-episcopal', with its own privileges and exempt from episcopal authority.

The church possesses a seal engraved with the legend *The Peculiar Jurisdiction of the Chapel in the Peak*" (the other side reads, "*The Seal of the Jurisdiction of St Charles the Martyr*"), and the registers call the chapel's ministers, "*Principal Official and Judge in Spiritualities in the Peculiar Court of Peak Forest.*"

The Dean and Chapter of Lichfield did attempt to gain some hold over this church, but were firmly rebuffed.

This independence from ecclesiastical authorities made the chapel popular with eloping couples – so much so that the registers contained a separate section for 'Foreign Marriages' (foreign here meaning from outside the parish rather than from outside the country). This continued until Parliament put a stop to it in 1804.

Pentrich, St Matthew

Various
The church of Pentrich was given by Ralph FitzStephen to Darley Abbey in 1175. After the dissolution of the monasteries, the church passed into the hands of the Zouch family and in 1634 into that of the Cavendishes. The Parliamentary Commissioners say of it: "Pantridge is a viccaridge (...) M[r] Robert Porter is viccar an able and pious man".

The lower tower and the nave arcades are late 13th century and the rest of the church belongs to the 13th – 15th century. The font is dated 1662, but appears to be partly Norman. This font was used, at one point, for the salting of beef in a church-warden's house, but it was recovered in the mid 19th century and returned to the church.

The area is known for the Pentrich Revolution of 1817, as recorded in the parish registers:

"On the evening of the 9th June an insurrection broke out in Pentrich, S. Wingfield, Swanwicke, and Ripley, which was quell'd next day at or in the neighbourhood of Kimbereley".

Cox notes that this incident was made use of by the vicar of Pentrich to argue for the building of a chapel of ease at Ripley, asserting that the smallness of the church "has occasioned a neglect of religious duties and morals, the lamentable effects of which during the last two years are but too well known, and have rendered it an imperious duty upon the well-disposed inhabitants to take some means for stemming the torrent of irreligion and disaffection." He seems to have got his way, as the Ripley church was built shortly after in 1821.

Pilsley, St Mary

19th century
1873 by S. Rollinson. Contains a reredos of Derbyshire marble.

Pinxton, St Helen

Various
This church may have been among those given to Burton Abbey by Wulfric Spott at the beginning of the 11th century. However the 13th century tower and the beginning of the nave are the oldest parts of the present building. A new church was built beside the medieval building in 1750, incorporating the old tower and chancel, and an aisle and porch was added in 1939.

At the time of going to print the church was undergoing restoration

Pleasley, St Michael

Perpendicular

The church is largely 13th century but has a Norman font and Norman chancel arch. The tower and its pinnacles were repaired with iron clamps and stays following an earthquake on the 17th March 1816. The steeple was also badly damaged and it was pobably as a result of this that it was subsequently removed. The church as a whole was restored in 1876.

The church registers contain the following entry:

"1664: A Blazzing Starr hath here appeared. Continueing its flames for aboute eight weekes past Eastward inclining to the North it did rise in the East and sett in ye West. Allmost in the line and nigh the same time of ye rising and setting.

1665: In this year after ye blazing starr was ye warr at sea with ye Hollanders & ye greate Plague at London & many other in this Nation. In London in this year there dyed of ye Plague above ninety thousands."

The Normon font

Quarndon, St Paul

19th century

Originally a chapel to All Saints, Derby, and of Norman origins, this church is mentioned in the *Inventory of Church Goods* in the reign of Edward VI. The Parliamentary Commissioners saID of it: "Quarne is a chapel apperteyning (to All Saints) two myles distant and may conveniently be united to Kedlestone it lying neare."

In 1697, difficulties in ensuring that regular services were held here led to the responsibility for this being divided between 16 clergymen of different parishes. It did not come to be regarded as a parish in its own right until the mid 18th century.

The church was demolished in 1872 and a new church by Giles & Brookhouse, was built on a different location in the village in 1874. The south doorway of the original church was Norman and well preserved until that time, but it did not survive the demolition.

At each upper corner of the tower are four figures depicting the four gospel writers – lion, eagle, bull and man, all with wings.

Renishaw, St Matthew

20th century

This was originally a chapel of ease for the Eckington parish. The present building by Naylor & Sale was built in 1903.

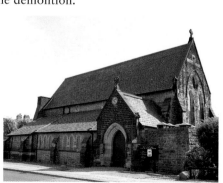

Radbourne, St Andrew

14th/15th century: Perpendicular

The first mention of a church at Radbourne (one of the manors of Henry de Ferrers) is during the reign of Henry III, and it was considered an *ecclesia* by 1291. Standing in the grounds of Radborne Hall, the building is mostly 14th and 15th century, with some earlier remnants, such as the late Norman double sedilia in the chancel. The tower is 15th century and the woodwork and benches are said to have come from Dale Abbey after its dissolution.

The church was repaired in 1844 and repewed at this time in such a way that the congregation sat with their backs to the altar, facing the pulpit and reading desk which were now set at the west end. It was again restored in 1889 by Chorley & Connon and the pulpit returned to a more conventional orientation.

The oak screen dates from the 1889 restoration.

John de la Pole d.1491 and his wife.

South nave window 1933 by Ernst Rinderspacher.

Repton, St Wystan

Anglo-Saxon and various
Repton was originally the capital of the Kingdom of Mercia and this church would have been the first Christian church built in the Midlands. Diuma, who came from Lindisfarne with three other priests to convert the kingdom to Christianity, was buried at Repton in 658, two years after his death.

The church was built on the site of an ancient abbey and dedicated to St Wystan (Wystan was a Mercian prince, assassinated by his brother Berfert). At the time of the Domesday Survey, Repton was said to have a church and two priests. The church was given to Calke Abbey in c1160 and the canons transferred from Calke to Repton in 1172.

The priory was destroyed in 1538 and its possessions plundered.

The Anglon-Saxon parish church was almost completely rebuilt around the beginning of the 14th century but the chancel, north and south east corners of the crossing, part of the transept and the crypt remain what Pevsner calls "one of the most precious survivals of Anglo-Saxon architecture in England". Some have dated the original church as early as pre-874. Rebuilding

of the aisles took place in the 13th century, followed by their being widened around 1340, when the tower and spire were added. The church was "beautified" in 1792 and restored in 1885 by A. Blomfield.

The Anglo-Saxon crypt. Thought to be the mausoleum of King Wiglaf in 840.

Riddings, St James

19th century: Gothic style
Built in 1832 by Francis Bedford who also built some of the London Waterloo churches. The chancel by F. C. Penrose was added in 1884. The west gallery stand on cast iron columns.

Ridgeway, St John the Evangelist

19th century: Gothic style
Built in 1838-40 by Woodhead & Hurst. The tower was added in 1883-4. Only the chancel is now in use for worship, the nave and aisles having been converted into a hall and meeting rooms.

Ripley, All Saints

19th century: Gothic style
A Commissioners' church built in 1820 at a cost of £1,600 and consecrated in 1821. It was enlarged in 1859-62 by Barber & Barber. The baptistery was added in 1921.

One of the main reasons for the building of this church was the alarm caused by the nearby 'revolution' at Pentrich in 1817 which was attributed by the vicar of that church to "a neglect of religious duties and morals" – which would have been exacerbated by the fact that the church at Pentrich had no free seats available for those who could not afford pew rents! (see Pentrich on p.139).

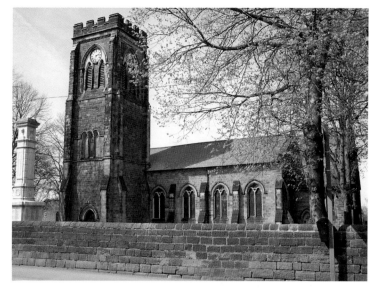

Risley, All Saints

16th/17th century
There may have been a chapel in Risley prior to the present church and Cox conjectures that this may have been a chapel to St Osyth or Scytha, which is mentioned in the *Valor Ecclesiasticus*. The location of this chapel is not certain.

The present church was built by Michael and Katharine Willoughby in 1593, but it was not consecrated until 1632. It is a rare example of an surviving Elizabethan church. The north aisle was added in 1841 when the church was repaired.

Rosliston, St Mary

19th century: Early English style
This was originally a chapelry of Walton and was mentioned in the Taxation Roll of 1291. The Parliamentary Commissioners described it as a "chapel apperteyning" to Walton, saying that "Rosliston (is worth) two and twenty pounds. Mr Salt is curate a frequenter of Alehouses and scandalous. Rosliston is remote from Walton and near to Caldwell and may conveniently be united to Caldwell."

A Brief was applied for in 1818, stating that the chapel was ancient and small, lacking in a chancel or room for the communion table so that "the Holy Sacrament cannot be administered with that decency and order which are so desirable". The chapel was thus taken down and replaced in 1819 with the present building by Thomas Stretton. The west tower and spire from the original chapel were allowed to remain, part of the spire having been rebuilt in 1802.

Cox notes that at the time of his visit, the old font had been "reversed and utilised as a chopping block".

Rowsley, St Katherine

19th century: Norman style
The church was built in 1855 by A. Salvin. The north aisle was added in 1859. The churchyard contains a 9th century Anglo-Saxon Cross head.

Sandiacre, St Giles

Norman and Decorated
There was a priest and a church at Sandiacre at the time of the Domesday Survey. The church was given to the cathedral of Lichfield to be under the care of the Prebendary of Sandiacre, who would have been responsible for the services — performed by himself and later by a chaplain.

The south doorway, nave and chancel arch are Norman, but there are also remnants of the original Saxon building. It has a very good 14th century chancel, which may have been given by Roger de Norbury, Bishop of Lichfield, and a 13th century tower.

By 1848, the church was in a very dilapidated condition. The chancel, which was boarded up at the time, was described as being "a lamentable spectacle of neglect and decay". The church was repaired throughout in 1855 and the chancel was restored in 1864 by Ewan Christian, for the Ecclesiastical Commissioners.

Sawley, St Mary

19th century tin tabernacle
A chapel of ease for All Saints, Sawley. This is one of the 'tin tabernacles' that were so popular during the time of rapid church expansion in the 19th century and probably dates from c1860. It is the only one left in the Derbyshire diocese still in use as a church.

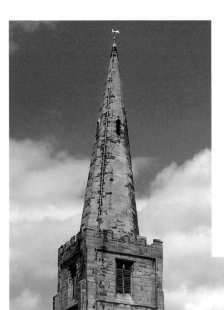

Sawley, All Saints

Various: Mainly Decorated
The Domesday Survey records that there was a priest and two churches in the manor of Sawley – these would probably have been Sawley and Wilne. However there is an even earlier record of Sawley when, in 822, Bishop Ethelwald of Lichfield appointed a Prebendary of Sawley, which until the 19th century was known as Sallow.

The chancel arch, which was restored in 1865 by an Ecclesiastical Commissioners architect, is Norman and the chancel is late 13th century. The arcades are late 13th and early 14th century, and the west tower is Perpendicular. The church was repaired and reseated in 1889 by Evans & Jolley.

Sawmills, St Mary

20th century
1902 mission room.

Scarcliffe, St Leonard

Various

The church was probably founded in the early 12th century when the advowson was given to Darley Abbey by Hubert Fitzralph. The south doorway and chancel doorway are Norman. The tower dates from the 13th century but was rebuilt in 1842. The tower had a spire but this became dangerous and was removed.

The church is notable for the 13th century effigy of Lady Constantia de Frechville (d.1175) with her child in her arms. Local legend has it that she and her baby were lost in the woods and, being in danger of death from exposure, were guided to safety by the church's curfew bell.

The building was restored in 1902 by Currey & Thompson and repaired in 1958–65 by Nye & Partners.

Scropton, St Paul

19th century: Mainly early English style/Decorated style

The Domesday Survey shows Scropton, one of the manors of Henry de Ferrers, as having a church and a priest. This church was replaced in the 13th century with a building which was again replaced in 1856 with one by B. Ferrey when it had become unsafe. The church retains the c.1510 tomb of Nicholas Agard, and opposite are the remains of the 600-year-old churchyard cross.

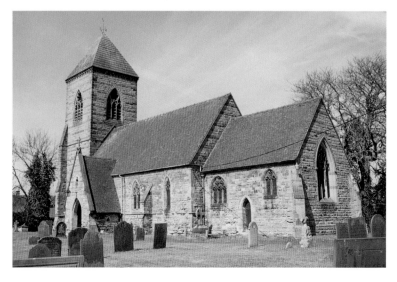

Shardlow & Great Wilne, St James

19th century: Gothic style
This church was built in 1838 at a cost of £6,000, probably by H. I. Stevens. Parish rooms were added in 1989 by A. Shaw.

Sheldon, St Michael and All Angels

19th century
There was a chapel here in the 15th century, but it was demolished and the present building of 1865 by S. Rollinson erected nearby. Cox mentions an unusual wedding that took place here:

"Last Saturday, at the chapel of Sheldon, in the High Peak of Derbyshire, were solemnised the nuptials of a widow gentlewoman of that place, of about 80 years of age, to a young lad (by the consent of his parents) of about 14." (from a list of Derbyshire events copied in 1776 from a parchment written around 1680).

Shirebrook, Holy Trinity

19th century
The church by Patterson & Hine, which dates from 1844, was enlarged in 1898-1904 by H.J. Price. The original building became the lady chapel, in the form of a south aisle to a new, spacious nave.

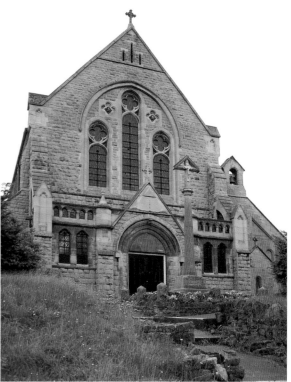

J.C. Cox

Shirland, St Leonard

Perpendicular
The first mention of this church in the historical records occurs in 1307, but there may have been a church on this site at an even earlier date. The present church is mainly Perpendicular in style and probably dates from around the middle of the 15th century.

Cox cites the following mention from the Terrier of Shirland, October 1795:- "the parson of Shirland receives from Sam. Lindley of Toadhole Furnace, which his predecessors have paid before him beyond the memory of man, a fat goose at Christmas, and a good gammon of bacon at Easter" (Lambeth MSS 944, no.28). Reseating was carried out in 1847- 49 by H.I. Stevens. The church was restored and repaired in 2004 by A. Short & Partners.

Shirley, St Michael and All Angels

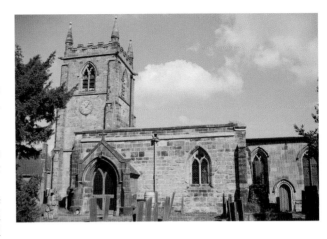

Various

Shirley was another of the numerous manors of Henry de Ferrers, and had a priest and a church by the time of the Domesday Survey. Of it, the Parliamentary Commissioners say: "Shirley is a viccaridge really worth thirtye pounds per annum. Mr Henry Salte viccar insufficient and scandalous."

In the east wall of the north aisle may be found a set of Norman carvings – a lintel depicting animals and

birds. The chancel is 14th century as is the south aisle, and the west tower and north aisle are 19th century. The tower was added sometime between 1817, when Godfrey Meynell made his drawing of it, and 1839 when *Stemmata Shirleiana* shows the tower. A north aisle was added in 1842, when the church was renovated and repaired by W. Evans and H.I. Stevens, at which time the only remaining Norman arch was removed. The tower was rebuilt by H. I. Stevens in 1861, owing to problems with its original construction.

Shottle, St Lawrence

19th century
1861.

Sinfin, St Stephen

19th century
This was built in 1935 by P. H. Currey.

Sinfin Moor, Sinfin Moor Ecumenical Church

20th century

This ecumenical church with its Anglican, Methodist and URC congregation was formed as a house church in 1972. The congregation moved to the present church centre in 1975. It is one of the first churches to have had an ecumenical congregation from the outset, rather than being formed from the amalgamation of existing churches. The building is used for community activities during the week.

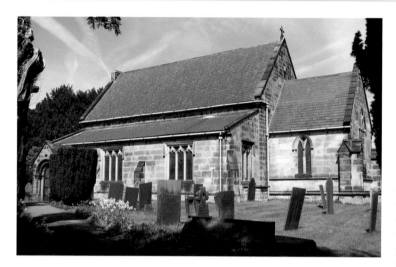

Smalley, St John the Baptist

Various

This was originally a parochial chapelry of Morley. The old chapel was built of light red sandstone, with repairs carried out in brickwork and a 15th century timbered roof. It apparently possessed a good quantity of stained glass. This church was replaced in 1793, though later alterations have left no trace of the 18th century building. Norman style transepts were added in 1844 and removed again in 1862 when the north and south aisles were added. A chancel was built in 1863 to replace the original apse. The west tower by Currey & Thompson is in the Arts and Crafts style with a pyramid top. The parish registers contain the following entry:

"1785. Dec 23. Samuel Ligget Buried. Poper,
(underneath, and in another hand)
Starved to death by the Humanity of the parish Officer."

To this is added on the facing page:

"The Poor Rates of this Township having very considerably increased, it was thought advisable to have a standing overseer and a meeting of the Parishoners was held to appoint a man to the office distinguished for extreme parsimony & hardness of heart. The result of the appointment was cruelty and oppression to the poor, and Samuel Liggat was absolutely starved to death. I was from home when he was buried, and did not know of his death until many months afterwards when, although I obtained sufficient information to convince me of the fact I could not obtain sufficient evidence to convict the overseer upon it, and therefore he escaped the punishment which he deserved."

R.W. (Robert Wilmot) Rector

Smisby, St James

Various

This was originally built as a chapel of ease in 1068 by the monks at Repton but was regarded as a parochial chapel by the 13th century and became a parish church in the 19th century.

In 1650, the Parliamentary Commissioners said of it that : "Smisby is a donative really worth thirtye pounds per annum. Mr Richard Mawson performs the cure and receives the profits to his owne use or one Mr Lees, both of them insufficient and scandalous."

A new nave and chancel were added between 1300-1350 by Joan Comyn of Smisby Manor and the original building became the south aisle. The font is 14th century and the windows are mainly 16th and 17th century. The church was restored in the 1890s and the floor was raised to accommodate heating channels – thus concealing the bases of the pillars. The linenfold panelling of 16th century design was taken from Ashby-de-la-Zouch castle in the mid 19th century. The font is 14th century and was moved to its present location during the 1890s restoration. Replacement of the roof and repairs were carried out in 2003 by A. Short & Partners.

The view from the church tower is said to have inspired Sir Walter Scott's *Ivanhoe*.

Snelston, St Peter

Mainly 19th century

Until the 19th century, Snelston was a parochial chapelry and in 1650, the Parliamentary Commissioners recommended that it even be made the parish church to replace Norbury.

The original church was probably of the 14th century, but of this nothing remains save for the chancel arch and the tower. It was rebuilt in 1825 and again in 1907 by Hodgson Fowler.

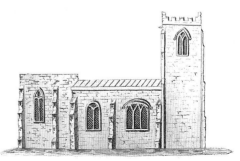

Somercotes, St Thomas

19th and 20th century
In 1852-54, work was undertaken to convert a Dissenting chapel into a chapel of ease. Robert Barber and Ewan Christian planned the conversion and added the chancel, side chapel and vestry. The remainder is by P.H. Currey in 1902. It was reconstructed following a fire in 1980, by Montague Associates of Derby.

Somersall Herbert, St Peter

Various
Somersall Herbert was among the manors held by Henry de Ferrers. There does not appear to have been a church here at the time of the Domesday Survey. The original church on this site was dedicated to St Blaise. It may have originally been a chapel of Sudbury and did not achieve independent stature until the 15th century.

The oldest part of the church is the font which probably dates to the 12th century. The church was rebuilt in 1836 and repaired again in 1874 by C.J. Neale. A tower was added in 1912. The 18th century porch from the earlier building still remains.

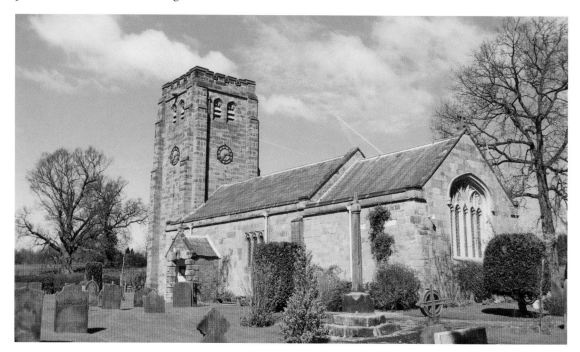

South Darley, St Mary the Virgin

19th century neo-Norman style
The church, by J. Mitchell, was built in the 1840s as a chapel of ease to St Helen's, Darley Dale, and it became a parish church in 1845. A chapel was added in 1866. The east window is by Morris & Co.

South Normanton, St Michael and All Angels

Various
The advowson of South Normanton, along with that of Pinxton, was sold by William le Wyne to Sir Alured de Solney in 1342. The church is not mentioned in the Domesday Book, but must date from shortly after as the oldest parts of the building are in the Norman style. The tower is 15th century and the nave and south aisle are from the 1878 restoration by Rollinson & Son.

South Wingfield, All Saints

Various

The Domesday Survey records South Wingfield as having a priest but no church. The church is first mentioned during the reign of Henry II (1154-1189) at which time it was given to Darley Abbey by Ralph Fitz-Stephen. The church, with its 13th century nave and c1360 chancel, was rebuilt in 1803 in the Classical style. It has a Norman tub font.

Spital, St Leonard

19th century

A mission church for St Mary and All Saints, Chesterfield

Spondon, St Werburgh

Decorated

The manor of Spondon had a priest and a church by the time of the Domesday Survey. In the reign of Henry I, 1154–1189, it was given by William de Ferrers to the Hospital of Burton Lazars in Leicester – the foremost and most wealthy leper hospital in England. The church continued in its possession until the dissolution of the hospital by Henry VIII. The Parliamentary Commissioners say it: "is a viccaridge really worth thirtye pounds per annum. Mr Saunderson vicar, able and of good conversation."

On the evening of Maunday Thursday 1340, a fire broke out in the church and not only destroyed the church itself and all its contents but spread to and destroyed almost the whole town – causing over £1,000 pounds of damage. It is almost certain that the church was rebuilt almost immediately after, but little of that church survived intact through to its rebuilding by T. Johnson in 1826 which resulted in what Cox calls "perhaps the most melancholy instance in Derbyshire of a good church spoilt."

Of the pre-1340 church, nothing remains save, perhaps, for lower parts of the tower. The church was restored again in 1891–92 by J. Oldrid Scott.

In the south wall is a small, somewhat mysterious low window, now blocked up, which may have served for distributing Communion to lepers, who would not have been allowed in the church itself. This seems especially likely given the fact that there was a chapel for lepers at nearby Locko.

There was a well near the church, known as the Holy Well, whose water was used for baptism at Spondon, Chaddesden and Stanley – part of the tradition that chapelries should use baptism water provided by the mother church.

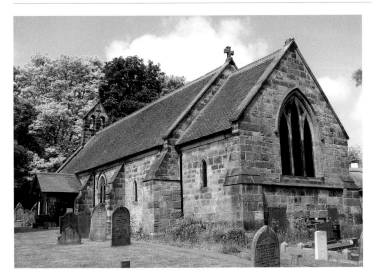

Stanley, St Andrew

19th century

The church was rebuilt in 1874 by Evans & Jolley, but still retains some Norman and 13th century remnants, such as the south door.

Stanley Common, All Saints

20th century
This was built in 1913 as a joint Anglican/Methodist church.

Stanton by Bridge, St Michael

Various
The 1650 Parliamentary Commissioners recorded that: "Stanton juxt Pont is a parsonage . . . noe chappell apperteyning". Judging from its Saxon and Norman remains, there had been a church here for a long time, although its early history is obscure. The chancel arch may be Saxon, although the chancel itself was probably rebuilt c1275. The rest of the church is likewise largely late 13th century but was rebuilt by the rector Augustine Jackson in 1683.

   Bassano's Church Notes (1710) records the following, inscribed with "a pensell" on the south chancel wall: "When thro ffanaticall prophanesses yᵉ past of yᵉ house of God was inhabited by Oroles [owls] and Spiders, it was thus rebuilt and beautyfyed for yᵉ use of Christians by Augustine Jackson rector of yᵉ church."

   The bellcote was of wood, until it was replaced with a stone one by Ewan Christian in 1865 when he carried out restorations and added the south porch.

Stanton by Dale, St Michael with All Angels

Mainly 14th century
This was one of the early possessions of Dale Abbey and remained entirely under its jurisdiction until the dissolution of the monasteries. The Parliamentary Commissioners say of it that "Stanton juxta Dale is a viccaridge really worth seven pounds per annum, the place is void, in a peculiar antiently an abbey, fitt to be united to Stanton and Stanton made a Parish Church." Cox points out that there is evidently some confusion here between Stanton and the chapel at Dale.

   The structure is mainly c1300, though the tympanum of the south doorway may be Norman. The tower is probably 15th century. There are three windows by Kempe. The church was repaired and restored in 1872, with the chancel being lengthened at this time.

Stanton in the Peak, Holy Trinity

19ᵗʰ century
1839.

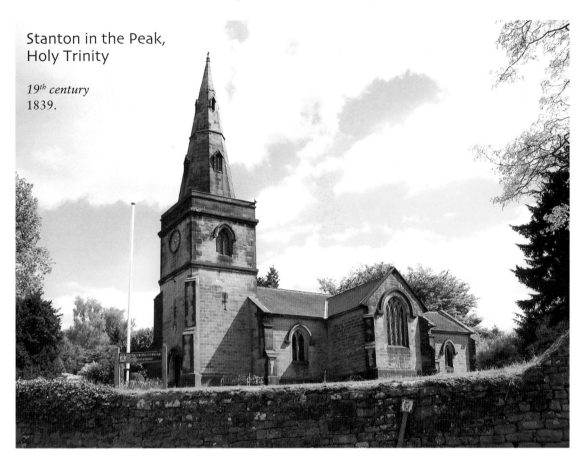

Stapenhill, Immanuel

20ᵗʰ century
The simple concrete church was opened in 1963 and given its own parish in 1996.

Stapenhill, St Peter

19th century: Decorated style

The church, along with the town of Stapenhill, was given to Burton Abbey in 1026-1150. The church achieved the status of a vicarage in 1255.

The Parliamentary Commissioners say of it that: "Stapnell is a viccaridge and hath a chappell at Caldwell apperteyning (. . .) Mr Lucas is vicar and of good conversation. Mr Thomas Salt is curate a frequenter of ale houses and a swearer."

A Brief was obtained to demolish and replace the original church in 1780 on the grounds that it was "a very ancient structure and greatly decayed". This does not seem to have been put into effect, beyond the replacement of the nave and demolition of the tower.

The church, apart from the chancel, was entirely rebuilt in 1837 by H.I. Stevens at the expense of the then vicar, John Clay, the chancel itself being removed in 1861 and the church enlarged. The church was again rebuilt in 1881 by Evans & Jolley. Tradition holds that the original church had many Saxon features, but these, if they existed, have been obliterated.

Staveley, St John the Baptist

Perpendicular

The Domesday Book records that the manor was held by Ascuit Musard and that there was a church and priest here at that time. Nothing is left of the original church except for the Norman font and some incised stones that form window sills in two south aisle windows. The west tower is 13th century, with battlements and pinnacles dating from 1681. The south aisle is Perpendicular, but the north aisle is by G.G. Scott and was added during the extensive restoration undertaken in 1865-9.

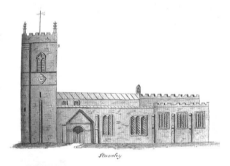

Staveley

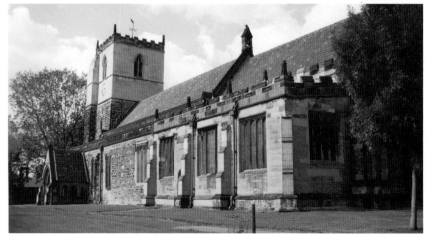

Steetley, All Saints

Norman (reconstruction)

Originally a chapelry of Whitwell, the church was probably built on the site of a Saxon wooden church, sometime in the reign of Stephen (1135-1154), by Gley de Briton or one of his sons.

Cox considers it to be "one of the most complete and beautiful specimens of Norman work on a small scale that can be met with anywhere in this country or in Normandy". Having fallen into decay by 1742, at which time it was used as a barn, it had been rebuilt in 1830 but soon reverted to a ruined state.

It was reconstructed by J.L. Pearson and reconsecrated in 1880. Pearson made efforts to retain as much of the Norman fabric as possible and to rebuild other parts in sympathy with the original. The result is quite extraordinary.

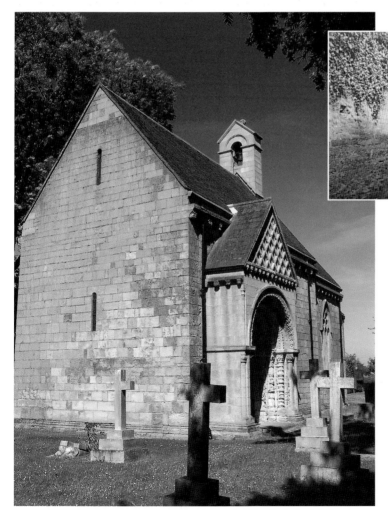

Above: J.C. Cox's photograph shows how ruined the chapel had become by the time of his visit in c1873.

Continued over leaf

Steetley, All Saints – continued

Above left: The apse.

Above right: This tomb slab is said to be that of Lawrence le Leche who, like the later and better known Mompesson of Eyam, refused to leave his flock during the plague of 1349. He died seven years later.

Left: The Thornton window by Alfred Fisher, 1990.

The south doorway.

Right: Detail from
south doorway.

Stonebroom, St Peter

19th century: Arts & Crafts
The church was designed by P.H. Currey and consecrated in 1907. The present tower is a small and stunted version of the original plan. The building was repaired in 1970-73 by Brian Taylor.

Stoney Middleton, St Martin

Mainly 18th century
This was originally a well-chapel built close to "three perpetual bubbling warm springs" as described by a Dr Short in 1734. A larger chapel may have been built here in the 15th century and the Parliamentary Commissioners in 1650 reported that it was a "parochial chapel thought fitt to be made a parish church."

The octagonal nave was added in 1759 after a fire in 1757 destroyed the previous nave. According to local legend, the first chapel was built in the 15th century by Joan Eyre (d.1463) as a thanksgiving for her husband's safe return from Agincourt. The tower certainly dates from this period. A memorial brass to Joan Eyre and her husband may be found in Hathersage church. The timber roof was replaced in 1861 and at this time the west doorway and windows were added to the tower.

Sudbury, All Saints

Various

There was already a church and priest at Sudbury at the time of the Domesday Survey. The south doorway may be Norman, but the church appears to have been thoroughly rebuilt in c1300 with further alterations in the 15th century. A new south porch was added in the 17th century. The church was enlarged in 1827 and heavily restored in 1874-

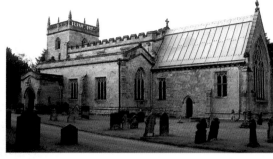

5. The Norman south doorway remains along with a small window in the chapel but both have been renewed.

The east window was given by Queen Victoria and Prince Albert, Queen Adelaide having lived at the hall.

The previous roof was stolen in the 1970s for its lead, and was replaced with felt. In 2000, new lead roofs to a newly designed style – Sudbury Delta Slot Vent – were installed by Mark Parsons of A. Short & Partners.

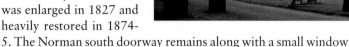

Sutton on the Hill, St Michael

Various

A church and a priest are mentioned here in the Domesday Survey for Sutton, one of the manors of Henry de Ferrers. Between 1162 and 1181, the church was given to Trentham Priory in Staffordshire.

This 14th century church was much rebuilt in 1863 by Giles & Brookhouse, leaving only the original tower (the spire was taken down and repaired in 1841 as the result of a lightning strike), the north aisle arcade and part of the chancel. A 14th century window which had for some time been bricked up and hidden by a 17th century monument, contains c1330 armorial glass.

The church registers contain the following passionate entry:

"1575: Richard Chreswell of Ashe died excommunicate the 6th of July about 10 of the clocke in the night and was buried the 9 of the same month lyke an Infidell without any Christian Ceremonie, only throughe great presumption of certayne yt favoured his error he was buried within the churchyard, the wch presumption although it was colored with manifest forgerie and by corporall othe mightelie defended, yet god who sitteth on heaven and beholdeth all things with the eye of his divine and perfect knowledge, beholding all the wayes of men and looking into the secret thoughts of their hearts doth see and heare their wicked imaginacons and counsels . . ." and so on at great length.

The monument to Judith Sleigh, d.1634, with a coffin carved in black stone.

The Churchwardens Accounts for the 1st July 1754 state that "Samuel Lygnes shall have Five shillings a year for the Whipping of dogs" (out of the church).

Sutton Scarsdale, St Mary

14th & 15th century

A church probably stood here as far back as the 12th century, although there are no remains of anything earlier than the 14th century in its fabric. It has a 14th century south porch and a 15th century Perpendicular tower. The church is much overshadowed by Sutton Hall that was built right up against it in 1740.

Cox records a local legend connected with this church:- A certain Sir Nicholas Leake went off to the Crusades, having first broken a ring in half, he and his wife keeping half each. He was taken prisoner by the Turks and held captive for many years, until he seemed to be on the brink of death. He therefore prayed to the Virgin Mary that he should be allowed to see Sutton again and vowed that if his prayer was granted he would provide for the poor in his parish. When he awoke the next morning, he found himself lying on the church porch of St Mary, Sutton. He was able to prove his identity, despite his much altered appearance, by showing his half of his ring to his wife. In fulfilment of his vow, he made provision in his will for eight bushels of wheat to be baked into loaves to be distributed to the poor. This custom appears to have still been in use as late as 1735.

Swadlincote, Emmanuel

19th century

This church was built in 1848 by H.I. Stevens.

Swanwick, St Andrew

19th and 20th century
Designed by Benjamin Wilson of Derby, the church was consecrated in 1860. The tower is from 1902 by Naylor, Sale & Woore and built at the expense of Fitzherbert Wright. The west window is by J.E. Nuttgens in 1953.

Swarkestone, St James

Various
The Parliamentary Commissioners recorded that: "Swarkstone is a parsonage really worth fiftye pounds per annum. Mr Samuel Bold Incumbent, disaffected formerly."

It was much restored by F. J. Robinson in 1874-6 as a consequence of some badly carried out alterations in 1828. The original church had Norman elements, but not much of the older church remains save for the tower and the Harpur chapel which contains 15th, 16th and 17th century effigies of the Harpur and Rolleston families.

Taddington.
St Michael and All Angels

Perpendicular/Decorated

This was one of the many Bakewell chapelries and probably existed at the time of the gift of Bakewell to the Dean and Chapter of Lichfield. The first mention of the chapel, however, is in 1280 and it was declared fit to be a parish in 1650 by the Parliamentary Commissioners. However it did not become so until 1890, having been made a perpetual curacy in 1748.

The present church dates from 1373 and was renewed in 1891 by Naylor & Sale. The registers call the east end of the south aisle the "Blackwall quire" and the east end of the north, the "Priestcliffe quire". The Priestcliffe quire was refurbished in 1923 and the Blackwall quire in 1943.

There is an ancient cross in the churchyard which Cox "would fain believe" to have been from the 7th century (due to its Celtic ornamentation) but which is dated by the National Schedule of Monuments to the 11th.

Cox also records how, on a visit to a public house nearby, he found the church's Norman font being used as a container for pea soup – it had reportedly been in use earlier as a washing up bowl for beer glasses. It has, fortunately, since been restored to the church. The Burlison & Grylls glass in the east window was added in 1993 and comes from the demolished church of St Peter, Birkenhead.

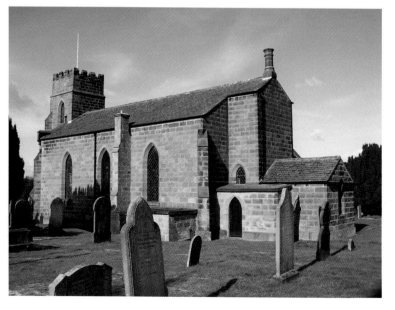

Tansley, Holy Trinity

19th century: Early English style

Built in 1839-40 by John Mason of Derby. The north aisle by Stevens & Robinson in the Gothic style was added in 1869. One of the south aisle windows contains a depiction of the archangel Uriel, by Ford Madox Brown (possibly 1862, but may be an early 1900s copy). The 1672 bowl of the font came from the St James' church in Derwent before it was submerged in the Ladybower Reservoir.

Temple Normanton,
St James the Apostle

20th century

The parish gets its unusual name from the fact that the manor was originally owned by the Knights Templar (first recorded in England in 1135) who retained possession until the order was repressed by Henry VIII. They briefly regained the manor during the reign of Mary, but subsequently lost it again. The chapel had a lintel stone with the date of 1623, but the actual foundation was probably much earlier, as indicated by the presents of some Norman style details. Unfortunately, this old chapel is nothing more than rubble now. The Victorian rebuilding by Rollinson & Son was followed by a wooden church built in 1922, which was replaced by the present, extraordinary yellow structure in 1986.

This fibreglass church owes its unusual design to the fact that it is situated over disused mines – which used to cause the previous building to shake alarmingly during services.

Fragments of the earlier buildings have been incorporated into the pathways around the church and piled up against the adjoining wall.

Thorpe, St Leonard

Various

Thorpe was a chapelry of Ashbourne at the time that the latter was given to Lincoln. However, it became an independent *ecclesia* sometime between 1291 and 1310. The tower is the oldest part, c1150 and the nave is Norman, but the chancel was rebuilt and extended in 1881 by F. Bacon. There is a 1767 sundial in the churchyard. It may be that the unusual 11th century tub font originally had figures inscribed, like those at Tissington.

The c1150 west tower.

Tibshelf, St John the Baptist

Various
The date of the foundation of this church is unknown but would probably have been during the reign of Richard I or John. The tower is 15th century, restored in 1729. Cox mentions that the south porch was once used as a coal-hole. The rest of the church is by Bodley & Garner 1887–8 and enlarged in 1908–11 by Currey & Thompson.

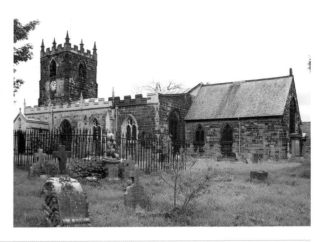

Ticknall, St George

19th century: Gothic
The first mention of a chapel at Ticknall appears c1200 in a charter concerning the exchange of land. The Parliamentary Commissioners in 1650 recorded that: "Ticknall, formerly a chapel and a member of Repton of late distinct of itself (. . .) South-Woods and Broade-stone also members of Repton, two myles distant and neare unto Ticknall may be united and Ticknall made a parish church."

In 1842 a new church by H. I. Stevens was erected, a good example of the Gothic Revival style. It has two windows by Morris & Co.

The original church, which had been dedicated to St Thomas á Becket, was blown up with gunpowder and its ruins may still be seen in the churchyard.

Tideswell,
St John the Baptist

Decorated, with Perpendicular tower

Tideswell was originally a chapel of Hope, at the time when the parish was handed over to the Dean and Chapter of Lichfield. It did not become a parish in its own right until the mid-13th century.

Known as "The Cathedral of the Peak", the church was built over a more or less unbroken period between c1340 and c1400, a fact which gives it its harmonious appearance.

The interior is notable for the carvings by Advent and William

Hunstone and by Tooley of Bury St Edmunds. The original chancel was replaced in 1360 and is now unusually high. The tower was added shortly after the completion of the church itself and the north aisle in 1625. The building was reseated in 1824–30 by R. Lane, restored by J.D. Sedding in the early 1870s and repaired in 1936 –39 by P.H. Currey.

J. C. Cox

Pew end by Tooley of Bury St Edmunds.

The chancel is almost as long as the nave and contains the tomb of Sir Sampson Meverell, a veteran of the Hundred Years War. The east window is from 1875.

Baptism – one of the pew ends by Advent Hunstone, part of a set depicting the seven sacraments.

Tissington, St Mary

Norman with neoNorman additions
Tissington was one of the chapelries of Bradbourne and given to the Priory of Dunstable in 1205. It is mentioned in the Annals of Dunstable in 1223. However there was probably a chapel on this site well before that date.

This Norman church was "reNormanised" in 1854, with the addition of the north aisle. The chancel arch is original Norman though partly covered over by the 17th century FitzHerbert monument.

The south doorway is Norman (though the porch is 19th century) with a tympanum containing two small standing figures, but the more interesting carvings are to be found on the Norman font.

The communion rail and the two-decker pulpit are c1600 and there are two mid-19th century windows showing the Flood and Noah's Ark.

Celtic and Anglo Saxon burial sites nearby indicate the very ancient nature of the site.

The Parliamentary Commissioners said of Tissington in 1650: "Tyssington is also a member of Bradbourne and a parsonage really worth fortye pounds per annum. Mr William Bott is curate, a man disaffected."

The communion rail and pulpit are c1600.

The Norman font.

The very primitive Norman tympanum.

I do set my bow in the cloud and it shall be for a token of a covenant between me and the earth

And the dove came in to him in the evening; and, lo, in her mouth was an olive leaf, pluckt off

The Noah window is mid-19th century, but the artist is unknown.

Trusley, All Saints

18th century: Classical
Trusley was one of the many estates given to Henry de Ferrers. There was no church here at the time of the Domesday Survey, though the advowson of such a church was given to Trentham Priory sometime in the first half of the 12th century. The church was replaced in 1713 with the present Wren style brick building, as recorded in the parish registers:

"The aforesaid sixth of August was ye opening of ye new Church, when we had both vocall and instrumental musick the service read as at Cathedrals an Anthem very well performed Mr Coke being one of ye performers. A Sermon preached by the Rector. Severall of ye gentry and clergy auditors of ye whole performance."

The baroque south porch may have come from elsewhere.

The box pews, communion rail and pulpit are all original.

Tupton, St John

19th century
Built in 1889–91, originally as a mission church in the North Wingfield parish.

Turnditch, All Saints

Various

The earliest mention of this church is in the report of the Parliamentary Commissioners in 1650, which recommended that Turnditch, being a chapel of Duffield, should be made a parish united to "Shottle, Posterne and Windley".

The south-east door gives a date of 1630, but Cox dates the walls as being as early as the 13th century. The font may be 15th century. The church was enlarged and the chancel replaced in 1882-4 by Giles & Brookhouse.

Twyford, St Andrew

Various

This was originally a chapel of Barrow, served by a chaplain appointed by the vicar of that church.

The church has a Norman chancel arch, 13th century tower, 14th century chancel, 15th century spire and nave rebuilt in the 18th century.

Unstone, St Mary

20ᵗʰ century
This was built in 1916-21 by Webster & Son and consecrated in 1920. The original plans included a tower, but this was never completed.

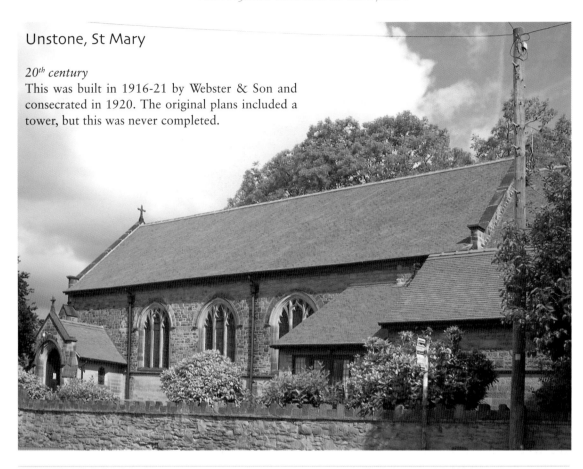

Upper Langwith, Holy Cross

Various
The church was given to the priory of Thurgarten (in Nottinghamshire) by Ralph Deincourt during the reign of Henry II (1154-1169).

The Norman chancel archway still remains, as does the Norman archway at the west end which was presumably for a tower which would have stood here. The chancel is 13ᵗʰ century with Perpendicular windows and the building was restored in 1877 by Norman Shaw who also added the bellcote.

Walton, St John

20th century
The older church, still standing, was replaced
by a modern building by J. W. Woore of Naylor
& Sale in 1916.

Walton on Trent, St Lawrence

Various
The church at Walton on Trent would probably have been built shortly after the Domesday Survey. The
Parliamentary Commissioners in 1650 said that "Walton is a parsonage and hath a chapel apperteyning at
Rosliston".

The church has Norman origins, with a 13th century chancel. Application was made in 1826 for a Brief
(now in the British Museum) for "the collection of moneys for the repair" of the church, which is described
as being over 400 years old and in a ruinous state. The Brief was for the replacement of some of the
windows, repairs to the south wall and the renewal of the roofs. The south transept is from 1334 and was
the Waley Chantry. The tower is c1400. The church was restored in 1905 by W. S. Weatherley and
repaired in 1953–54 by Naylor, Sale & Widdows.

by J.C. Cox

Wessington, Christ Church

19th century:
  Early English style
The church was built in 1859 by Flockton & Son, and reordered in 1995 to improve facilities.

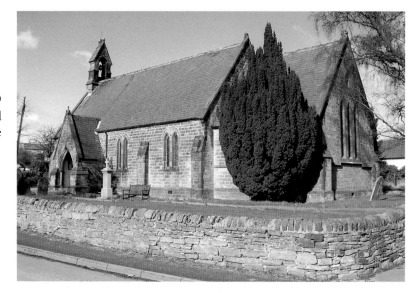

West Hallam, St Wilfrid

14th century: Decorated
A 14th century church with a 15th century tower. It was rebuilt in 1855 by G. G. Place.

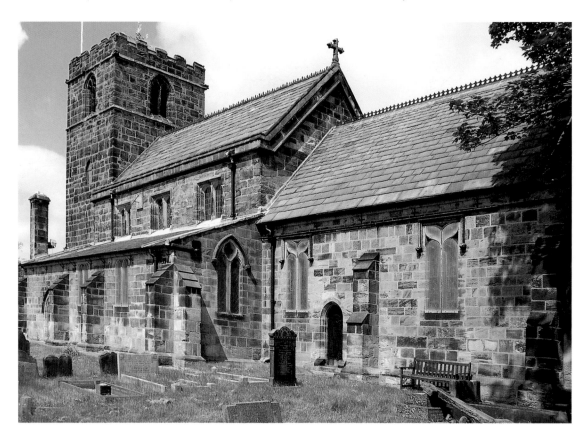

Weston on Trent, St Mary the Virgin

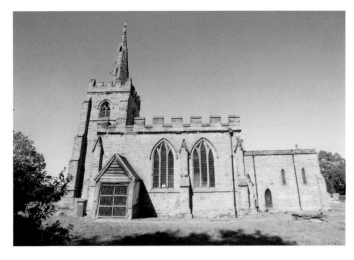

13th century: Early English
The Domesday Survey records that the Royal manor of Weston on Trent had two churches, Weston and Aston. The advowson of the church was given to Chester Abbey around 1175.

The Parliamentary Survey records that: "Weston super Trent is a parsonage really worth one hundred and twenty pounds per annum noe

chappell apperteyning. Mr John Boylstone Incumbent an able preacher and of good conversation."

There are no Saxon or Norman remains in the church, although there is some unusual, possibly unique in Derbyshire, geometric tracery in the east window. The building is 13th century with 14th century north aisle windows. The half-timbered porch is 17th century as are the font and pulpit.

The 17th century half-timbered porch.

Whaley Thorns, St Luke

19th century
Built in 1879 by J.B. Mitchell-Withers

Whitfield, St James

19th century

The church was built in 1844 by E.H. Shellard, and consecrated in 1845. The chancel was enlarged in 1897 by Naylor & Sale. The south aisle window is by Morris & Co and designed by Burne-Jones.

Whitfield, St Luke

20th century: Gothic

This church began as a missionary daughter church for St James' (above), and started its life in a room over a local shop. In 1895, the congregation moved into a building on the present site, which was known as the "Iron Church" due to its being made of tin. This was removed in 1903 and building started on a new church in 1905 at the expense of Anne Kershaw Wood, the builder being Joseph Howard. The church was completed and dedicated in 1906. The east window was added in memory of Anne Kershaw Wood.

Whittington, St Bartholomew

19th century

There was a church on this location at least as early as 1140. The medieval church was replaced in 1863 by a new building, which was destroyed, apart from its tower, by a fire in 1895. The new church by E. R. Rollinson, incorporating the tower and with a higher roof and a clerestory was opened in the following year.

Whitwell, St Lawrence

Norman and Decorated

The Domesday Book records a church and priest for the manor of Whitwell. This cruciform building has a Norman west tower and west door. The masonry of the nave and chancel are also Norman. The clerestory is a rare example of its kind, its Norman character being entirely preserved. The chancel was enlarged in the first half of the 14th century and transepts were added at this time. There was also, at one point, a Norman tympanum over the chancel door with 'Norman circles' and a dragon.

The church was restored by J. L. Pearson in the 19th century.

Willington, St Michael

Early English

Although there is no mention of a church here at the time of the Domesday Survey, William the Conqueror gave the church at Willington to Burton Abbey in 1185. It passed soon after into the hands of the Willington family, who later (1223) gave it to the Repton Priory. It was classed as an *ecclesia* in the Taxation Roll of 1291, but soon afterwards it became a vicarage, with its tithes going to the Priory.

The church reverted to the Crown after the dissolution of the monasteries and thence into the hands of Sir John Port, the founder of Etwall Hospital and Repton School.

The Parliamentary Commissioners said of it: "Willington is a viccaridge really worth five pounds per annum. A small parish and neare to Finderne may be conveniently united to Findern and make one parish and the church sett at an equal distance betwixt both."

The tower was built in 1824 at a cost of £80 and the north transept was added not much later. The south doorway is Norman and the Norman chancel arch survived until 1824. The south nave windows are of the 19th century.

Wilmorton, St Andrew with St Osmund

20th century:
 Late Victorian Gothic Revival
This was built in 1904 by Currey & Thompson and consecrated in 1905. The first priest of this church was Lancelot Sydney Currey, brother of P.H. Currey.

St Osmund was the first bishop of Salisbury and is supposed to have completed the cathedral of Old Sarum. He is said to have been closely related to William the Conqueror and died in 1099.

Wilne, St Chad

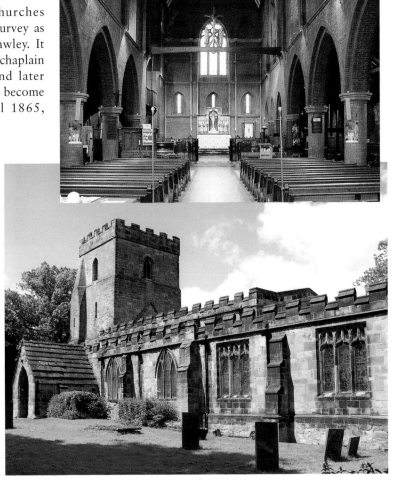

Mainly Decorated
This is one of the two churches mentioned in the Domesday Survey as belonging to the manor of Sawley. It would have been served by a chaplain appointed by the Prebend and later the vicar of Sawley. It did not become an independent parish until 1865, although it had parochial rights as early as 1822.

The church is largely 14th and 15th century, with the south aisle added in 1624 to accommodate a family chapel for the Willoughby family. It was restored by Currey & Thompson after a fire in 1917. The lower part of the west tower is 13th century, the clerestory 15th century. The font has Saxon carvings of a cross, dragons and birds and may be the oldest of its kind in Derbyshire.

Wingerworth, All Saints

Norman & 20th century

The original Norman church dates from early 12th century. A rood loft, the only example in Derbyshire, stands above the chancel arch whose inner surface is decorated with medieval wall paintings. There are Early English lancet windows in the chancel.

In 1963-64, the church was massively extended and the original nave was converted into a narthex for the new nave by Naylor, Sale & Widdows, built with concrete arches and a semicircular apse. Along each side of the new structure are long windows with abstract stained glass by Pope & Parr.

The 1964 nave.

The inside of the chancel arch is painted with the head of Christ and four saints – probably dating from the late 12th century.

This is a rare surviving example of a rood loft. It is attached to the wall above the Norman chancel arch of the original building, which now forms the narthex to the new nave. The later opens out from the north wall of the original church as can be seen to the left of this photograph.

189

Winshill, St Mark

Various
The south door is Norman, though the tower is 1824 as are the north transept and the nave and chancel ceilings.

The Parliamentary Commissioners said of it in 1650: "Winsell is a hamlet in the parish of Burton butt remote and may conveniently be vnited to Newton Soonye".

Winster, St John the Baptist

18th & 19th century
This was one of the chapels of Youlgreave, given along with that church to the Abbey of Leicester, in the reign of Henry II. The church was completely rebuilt in 1842 by Habershon, although the tower appears to date to 1721. It has an old and interesting font, remarkably well preserved, which Cox dates to c1200.

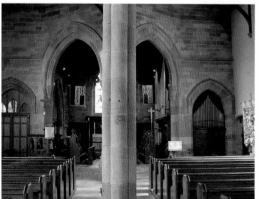

The church was altered again in 1883, by A. Roland Barker, leaving the church with its unusual layout of two aisles, divided by slim columns down the middle. The chancel south window is by Burne-Jones dating from 1887.

Wirksworth, St Mary the Virgin

Various.

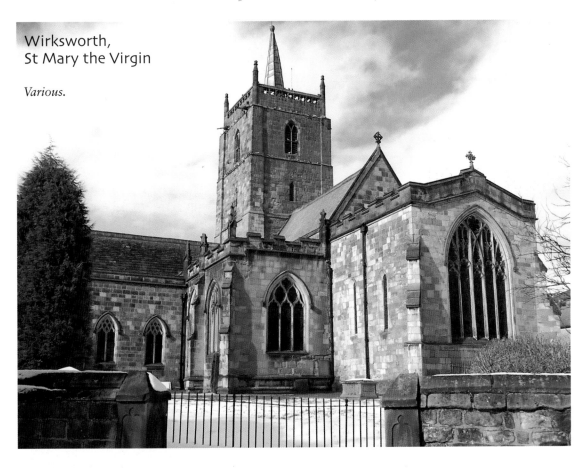

According to the Domesday Survey Wirksworth already had a church and priest, and it seems that there was already one here by the time of Edward the Confessor. The church and its chapels were given to the Dean and Chapter of Lincoln by Henry I. This was a wealthy and valuable holding due to the lead mining in the area and much has been spent on the church over the centuries.

There are only fragments of the Saxon and Norman churches that stood on this site. The Norman church was probably a large, cruciform one of similar size and shape to the present building which is mainly of the 13th–15th centuries. The church was much altered in the 19th century, first in 1820 and then enlarged in 1855 at which time the south porch was rebuilt and a new arch put into the chancel, dividing it in two. The following restoration, carried out in 1870 under the direction of George Gilbert Scott and at a cost of nearly £10,000 seems to have been largely concerned with getting rid of the effects of the 1855 restoration which had damaged the internal proportions of the building.

The attractive and unobtrusive north aisle screens were added by A.Short & Partners to provide space for a vestry and toilets.

J. C. Cox.

Continued over leaf

Wirksworth,
St Mary the Virgin – continued

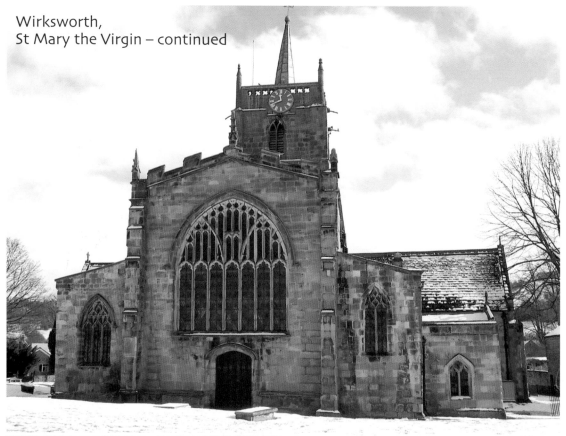

The massive 12th century font.

The 1909 north transept window is by Morris and Burne-Jones for Morris & Co.

Some Norman, possibly Saxon fragments built into the wall of the north transept.

Alabaster monument to Anthony Gell.

The most outstanding of the ancient fragments is a Saxon coffin lid of c800, showing the life of Christ.

Wormhill, St Margaret of Antioch

Late Decorated

Permission was given to erect a chapel at Wormhill in 1273, though the inhabitants were still required to attend the mother church at Tideswell on the major festivals.

The Parliamentary Commissioners in 1650 recommended that Wormhill should be made a parish with a number of surrounding hamlets. Wormhill became an ecclesiastical parish in 1859.

The base of the tower is medieval, but the rest was largely rebuilt and restored in 1864 by T. H. Rushforth. The font is of Sicilian, Kynance and Derbyshire marble.

The church registers contain the following rueful entry:

"1674, Nicholas Bagshawe, clerke and schoolmaster, for want of a better."

Also known as Marina or Marine, St Margaret is supposed to have been a Christian virgin of the 3rd of 4th century who came from Pisidian Antioch in Asia Minor. Having been thrown out of her home on account of her conversion, she was tortured by the Roman governor after she rejected his advances. In prison, the story goes, she was swallowed by Satan in the form of a dragon, but the cross she carried so irritated him that he spat her out. She is thus sometimes depicted as emerging from a dragon's mouth (as on the tympanum at Ault Hucknall) or as one of the dragon slaying saints along with St Michael and St George. She is the patron saint of women (especially in pregnancy and childbirth), nurses and peasants. She was one of the most popular saints in England in the 9th century and is supposed to be one of the saints who spoke to Joan of Arc. There are 200 churches in England dedicated to her.

Above: The transept was added by Garlick & Flint in 1904-10.

Below: Pew ends by Advent Huntstone.

Yeaveley, Holy Trinity

19th century

Yeaveley was originally a chapelry of Shirley and of it the Parliamentary Commissioners said in 1650:

"Yevely is a member and hath a chappell decayed and may conveniently be united to Hedlestone."

This original chapel fell into disuse and became ruined. A plain building was later built, and replaced in 1840. This new church, by J. Smith, was financed in part by the Incorporated Society and was opened on the 22nd May 1840, although it was not consecrated until 15th April 1841. The east window is in memory of the fallen of World War I and depicts St George and Joan of Arc. The church retains the medieval font from the original building.

Youlgreave, All Saints

Various

The church at Youlgreave was given to the Abbey of St Mary at Leicester, along with its chapels (Elton, Winster, Middleton, Gratton and Stanton, of which the last two have since vanished) probably sometime in the 12th century. A chantry was founded in the church towards the end of the 15th century.

Pevsner calls this "one of the most impressive churches of Derbyshire". Norman remains show that the church was built between 1130 and 1150, although there is no mention of it in the Domesday Survey. The south arcade is late Norman but the south door is probably later. The windows are mostly Perpendicular. The church appears to have been partially rebuilt and enlarged throughout in the 15th century, at which time the tower was added. The clerestory windows are 17th century though they may be early Tudor as this is the date of the nave roof.

The building was restored in 1869-70 by R. Norman Shaw. The north aisle has a window made up of fragments of medieval glass brought back from the ruined cathedral at Ypres.

The church possesses an exceptionally complete set of church registers going back to 1558 as well as Churchwardens' accounts from 1604 onwards and accounts of the constables and overseers of the poor, 1713-1754, which recorded such national events as the death of "Our most gracious soveraigne Lady Elizabeth quene of Englande, France and Ireland 1602 March 23", as well as the following samples which give a vivid picture of life at their time:

J.C. Cox

"1615 – A DRY SUMMER
There was no rayne fell upon the earth from the 25th day of March until the 2nd day of May, and there was then but one shower; after which there fell none tyll the 18th day of June, an then there fell another; after yt there fell none at all tyll the 4th day of August, after which tyme there was sufficient rayne upon the earth; so that the greattest pt of this land, specially the south p's were burnt upp, both corne and

Continued over leaf

hay. An ordinary Sumer load of hay was at 2li. and little or none to be got for money."

We also find such items as the sum of 1s 4d paid to Robert Walton for "whipping yᵉ dogges forth of yᵉ churches in tyme of divine service"; 2 shillings for a "strange preacher" in 1611 and 1 shilling in 1623 for a "pore boy which had his legg cut of".

The Constable's Accounts record 6 pence in 1706 "For a warrant to raise souldjers"; 6 pence in 1708 "Spent in raising Carriages for yᵉ souldiers that marched thro Winster;" 1s 6d in 1710 "Spent in search for Soldiers" and 6 pence "Given to Valentine Greaves who received a wound by Jer. Gregory when he was about seizing him for a soldier".

The Overseer of the Poor's accounts records the trials of ordinary life with such entries as the 1s 6d spent in 1726 "about Hellen Ley being Lunatick on yᵉ men that assisted George Clark to break yᵉ door being fast bolted on yᵉ inside supposing she had been dead." and the 2 shillings in 1752 "Given to Richᵈ Swindell that day he had his fingers cut of."

Alabaster panel to Robert Gylbert, d.1492 and his wife and family.

The interesting monument to Thomas Cokayne stands in the middle of the chancel. It is unusually small, probably because he was young at the time of his death.

Right: The east and chancel south windows are by Burne-Jones (1876 and 1897) and the north aisle east and nave south windows are by Kempe.

Below left: The font is c.1200 with a highly unusual side stoup brought from Elton church in 1838.

Below right: Small Norman sculpture in the north wall of the nave.

Appendix

A Letter Recounting the Storm of 1545

Wellbeloved sonne I recommend me unto you, gevyng you Godds blessing and myne. Son this is to sertifie you of soch straunge newes, as that hath of late chaunsed in these p'ties; that is to wytt, apon Satterday last past, being the 20th daye of this moneth, on Say~te Albons day, we had in these p'tyes great tempest . . . . .wether, about xi of the clok before none: & in the same tempest, The dev[ill] as we do suppose beganne in Nedewood, wch is ix myles from Da[rbie]; & there he caste down a great substance of wood; & pulled up by the rotts: & from thens he came to Enwalle [Etwall] wher at one M[re] Powret [Porte] doth dwell, & there he pulled downe ij great elmes, that there was a dossyn or xvj bode apon a piese of them; & went to the church and pullyd up the leade, & flonge it apon a great elme that standyth a payer of butt lengthes from the church & . . . . . . it hangyed upon the bowys like stremers; & afte . . . . . . tourned . . . . . . & the groundsells upward & some layd bye apon . . . . . . .heape & . . . . . .that was apon vij bayes long he set it a . . . . .gge & and the . . . . .ro[ots] sett upwards; & he hathin the same town left not past iiij or v housses hole. And from thence he came a myle a this side, & ther grewe apon lx or iiijxx wyllowes & apon xij or xvi he had brokyn in the mydds, & they were as great as a man's body: & so he lefte them lyke a yard and a half hye: And from thence he went to Langely, w[ch] is lyke iij myles from Darby & there he hath pullyd down a great p'te of the church, & rowled up the leade & lefte it lyeing, & so went to Syr William Bassets place in the same [towne] & all so rente it, & so pullyed a great parte of it down wth his . . . . & the wood that growethe abowte his place, & in his parke he pulled downe his pale & dryve out his deare, & pulled downe his woods, & so[me] brokedn in the mydds that was xvj or xx loode of wood of some one tree. And after that he went into the towne to Awstens housse of Potts & hath slayne his sonne & his ayer, & perused the hole towne, that he left not past ij hole howsses in the same towne. And from thence he went to Wy~dley lane & there a nourse satt w[t] ij children upon her lappe before the fyre, & ther he flonge downe the sayde howse, & the woman fell forwards ap[on the] yonge chyl[dren] afore the fyre, & a piese of timber fell apon her . . . . . .& so killed [her] but the children were saved & no more hurte [and none] of the house left standyng but the chimney, & there as the house stode, he flange a great tre, that there is viij or x lood of wood apon it. And from thence he went to Belyer [Belper] & there he hath pullyd & rent open xl houses; & from thence he went to Belyer [Belper] wood & he hath pullyd down a wondrous thyng of wood & kylled many light; & from thens to Brege [Heage] & there he hath pullyd down the chappyl & the moste part of the towne; & from thens to Wynfeldman that is the Erle of Shrowseberys & in the parke he pulled downe a lytell . . . .& from thens to Manfyld in Sherwood & there I am sure he hath done [no] good, & as it is sayd he hathe donne moche hurt in Chesshire & . . . . .shire. And as the noyse goeth of the people there felle in some places hayle stons as great as a mans fyste & some of them had prints apon them lyke faces. This is trewe & no fables, there is moche more hurt done besyds, that were to moch to wryte; by the reporte of them that have sene it; and thus fare you well.

From Lysons, Derbyshire, pp. 160-161.

The main architects of Derbyshire churches and examples of their work

Ambler, L., *St Mary Magdalene*, Creswell, 1899; restoration, *St Mary*, Bolsover, c1897.

Anthony Short & Partners, repair, *St John the Baptist*, Boyleston, 1981.

Arden, E., bellcote, *St James*, Edlaston, 1900.

Barber, Robert *St James*, Codnor, 1843; conversion, *St Thomas*, Somercotes, 1854 **& Barber, Samuel John** (1828-1890), enlargement, *All Saints*, Ripley, 1859 –1862.

Barry, Thomas Denville, (1815-1905) *Holy Trinity*, Erewash, 1851.

Bedford, Francis, *St James*, Riddings, 1832.

Blacking, William Henry Randoll (1889-1958), *Christ Church*, Litton, 1926-7; aisles, *St John the Evangelist*, Newbold, 1957.

Blagney, J.B., extension, *St Mary*, Chinley 1957-72.

Blomfield, Arthur, *St Werburgh*, Derby, 1892-4.

Bodley, George Frederick (1827-1907)
G. F. Bodley was a pupil of G. G. Scott (see below), one of the great architects of the Gothic revival.
Enlargement, *St Peter*, Hartshorne, 1901; extension, *All Saints*, Kedleston, 1907-13 **& Garner**, restoration, *Holy Trinity*, Kirk Ireton, 1885, *St John the Baptist*, Tibshelf, 1887-8; *St Michael and All Angels*, Kirk Langley, 1885.

Bonomi, Ignatius (1787-1870)
Christ Church, King Sterndale (with J. A. Cory).

Brocklesby, John Sydney (1879-1955), *St Andrew*, Langley Mill, 1911-3.

Brooks, James Martin (1852-1903), extension, *St Giles*, Killamarsh.

Butterfield, William (1814-1900)
William Butterfield, whose most famous works include *All Saints* Margaret Street and Keble College, Oxford, was one of the important architects of the Gothic Revival, also known as the Oxford movement, in England. He also designed the Anglican Cathedral in Melbourne, Australia. His works show a high degree of liturgical correctness and a rich, colourful originality.
Restoration, *St Leonard*, Monyash, 1887; *St John the Baptist*, Bamford, 1860; restoration, *St Michael and All Angels*, Hathersage, 1849-52; restoration, *All Saints*, Heath, 1882-6; restoration and addition of tiled floor, *St John the Baptist*, Ault Hucknall, 1885-8.

Caroë, W. D., restoration, *All Saints*, Breadsall, 1915.

Chantrell, R.D., *St George*, New Mills, 1830.

Charlewood, Henry Clement (1857 –1943), *SS Augustine*, Chesterfield 1931.

Charlewood, George Edward (1890 –1962), enlargement, *SS Augustine*, Chesterfield 1931.

Christian, Ewan (1814-1895) conversion, *St Thomas*, Somercotes, 1852.

Cockbain, H., *St Anne*, Miller's Dale, 1879; *Charles, King and Martyr*, Peak Forest 1876-7; *St Anne*, Over Haddon, 1880; restoration, *St Anne*, Beeley, 1882-4; *St John the Evangelist,* Cressbrook, c1897.

Coke-Hill, A., *St Barnabas*, Derby, 1880.

Comper, Sebastian, retro-choir, *Derby Cathedral of All Saints*; extension, *St Peter*, Littleover; enlargement, *St Mary*, Boulton by Derby, 1960.

Currey, Henry, (1820-1900)
restoration, *St Giles*, Hartington, 1860; *Christ Church*, Burbage, 1860; restoration (with **John D. Simpson**), *St John the Baptist*, Chelmorton and Flagg, 1868-1875.

Currey, Percy Heylyn, (1864-1942)
Canopy, *St Anne*, Derby, 1871; (*St Bartholomew*, Ilkeston, 1895-redundant); *St Stephen*, Borrowash, 1899; *St Thomas*, Somercotes, 1902; *Christ Church*, Holloway, 1903; *St Osmund*, Wilmorton, 1904; *St Mary the Virgin*, Ilkeston 1909-10; *St John the Evagelist*, Ilkeston, 1912; *St Osmund*, Derby; *St Steven*, Sinfin, 1935; repair, *St John the Baptist*, Tideswell, 1936-39; repair, *All Saints*, Bradbourne, 1938-1947.
& Thompson, Charles Clayton, enlargement, *St John the Baptist*, Tibshelf, 1908-11; *St Mary*, Buxton, 1914-15; *St Chad*, Wilne, 1917; *St Bartholomew*, Derby.

Dawes, William (1840-1897), *Holy Trinity*, Edale, 1885-6.

Devey, George, restoration *All Saints*, Sudbury, 1874-5.

Duesbury, Henry (alterations, *St John the Baptist*, Longford, 1843.

Duke, R.R., chancel, *St Michael and All Angels*, Earl Sterndale, 1877.

Eaton, Arthur, *St Edmund*, Allenton, 1939.

Evans(Robert) & Jolley (William), restoration, *St Wilifrid*, Egginton, 1891; restoration *St Michael and All Angels*, Breaston, 1895; *St Andrew*, Stanley, 1874; repairs and reseating, *All Saints*, Sawley, 1889.

Ferrey, Benjamin, Vice President of the Royal Institute of British Architects, (1810-1880), *St Paul*, Scropton, 1856; roof, *St Mary*, Crich, 1860-61.

Flockton, William, (1804-1864), **& Son (Thomas James Flockton, 1825-1899),** repairs and reseating, *St John the Baptist*, Dronfield, 1853-56; *St John the Evangelist*, Newbold, 1857; *Christ Church*, Wessington, 1859.

Fowler, Hodgson, rebuild *St Peter*, Snelston, 1907.

Garlick and Flint, transepts and chancel, *St Peter*, Fairfield, 1902.

Gibbs, James, Pupil of Christopher Wren, *St Mary*, Mappleton, early 18th century; nave, *Derby Cathedral of All Saints*, c1725.

Giles, William Giles, chancel, *St John the Evangelist*, Derby, 1871
& Brookhouse, *St Paul*, Quarndon, 1874; enlargement and restoration, *All Saints*, Turnditch, 1882-4; *St Giles*, Normanton by Derby, 1861.

Goodwin, Francis, *St John the Evangelist*, Derby, 1826-7.

Habershon, Matthew, *St Peter*, Belper, 1824; *Christ Church*, South Derby, 1838-41; *St John the Baptist*, Winster, 1840-2.

Hadfield, C.M., nave and chancel, *All Saints*, Glossop, 1923; enlargement, *St Andrew*, Hadfield 1923.

Hamilton, George Ernest, *St Michael and All Angels*, Earl Sterndale, 1828-9

Healey, T.H. & F., *All Saints*, Matlock Bank, 1884.

Hicks, Henry Leicester, (1881-1947), *SS Augustine*, Chesterfield, 1931.

Hill, A. Coke, *St Anne*, Ambergate, 1897.

Hine, Thomas Chambers (1813-1899), rebuild *St Martin*, Alfreton, 1868; *Holy Trinity*, Brackenfield, 1856-7; *St Paul*, Hasland, 1850-1.

Hodkin, Daniel, *St Werburgh*, Blackwell, 1827-8.

Holden, J., chancel, *St James*, Codnor, 1888-9.

Hugall, John West (fl. 1849-78), south aisle and chancel, *All Saints*, Lullington.

Hunt, Frederick William Hugh (d. 1921), *St Anne*, Derby, 1871.

Hurst, William (1787-1844), **& Woodhead, John** (d. c1838), enlargement, *SS Peter and Paul*, Eckington; *St John the Evangelist*, Ridgeway, 1838-40.
& Hurst, apse and vestry, *St Bartholomew,* 1966-9.

Johnson, Thomas, *St Matthew*, Overseal, 1840-1; restoration and enlargement, *St Werburgh*, Spondon, 1826.

Mason, John, *Christ Church*, Hulland, 1838; *Holy Trinity*, Tansley, 1839-40; west end, *St Mary*, Boulton by Derby, 1840; repair, *St Peter*, Chellaston, 1841; enlargement, *All Saints*, Ockbrook, 1835.

Milburn & Partners, *St Philip*, Chaddesden, 1954-6; *St Francis*, Mackworth, 1953-4.

Mills & Murgatroyd, *Holy Trinity*, Dinting Vale, 1875.

Mitchell, Joseph, *St John the Baptist*, Charlesworth, 1848-9; *St Michael and All Angels*, Brimington, 1847; *St Thomas*, Brampton, 1846-48.

Mitchell-Withers, John Brightmore (1837-1894), *St Luke*, Whaley Thorns, 1879; tower, *St Werburgh*, Blackwell, 1878.

Moffatt, William Bonython (1812-1887), *Holy Trinity*, Milford, 1848.

Montague Associates, reconstruction, *St Thomas,* Somercotes, 1980; modernisation, *St John the Evangelist*, c1972.

Moore, Leslie Thomas, (1856-1920), tower repairs, *St Mary and All Saints,* Chesterfield, 1933-34.

Moore, Temple Lushington, (1883-1957), tower repairs, *St Mary and All Saints,* Chesterfield, 1933-34.

Murta, Kenneth, *St Lawrence*, Heanor, 1981-2.

Naylor & Sale, restoration, *St Michael and All Angels*, Taddington, 1891; chancel, *St Thomas,* Brampton, 1891; enlargement, *St James*, Whitfield; restoration, *St John the Evangelist*, 1902, chancel, *St Michael and All Angels*, Brimington 1847; *St Augustine*, Derby; *All Saints*, Marpool, 1908; *St Matthew*, Renishaw, 1900-1909.
& Widdows, extension, *All Saints*, Wingerworth, 1963-64; *St Alkmund*, Derby, 1967-72; repair, *St Laurence*, Walton on Trent, 1953-54; roof, *All Saints*, Breasall, 1958-59.

Neale, Charles James, *St Peter*, Somersall Herbert, 1874.

Newton, Thomas, *Holy Trinity*, Middleton by Wirksworth, 1838.

Nicholson, Charles, *St John the Evangelist*, Long Eaton, 1922.
& Parker & Unwin, *St Andrew*, Barrow Hill, 1893-5.

Nye, David Evelyn (1906-1986), *Holy Trinity*, Middleton by Wirksworth, 1838
    & Partners, *St Paul*, Scropton, 1856; repairs, *St Leonard*, Scarcliffe, 1958-65.

Ogden & Wood, repair, *All Saints*, Bradbourne, 1947-50.

Parker & Unwin, *St Andrew*, Barrow Hill, 1893-95.

Paxton, J., restoration, *St Anne*, Baslow, 1852-53.

Peacock, J., *St James*, Derby, 1867; *St Thomas the Apostle*, Derby, 1881.

Pearson, J. L, *All Saints*, Steetley, 1880.

Preston & Vaughan, chancel, *St George*, New Mills, 1898.

Price, Hedley John (d.1905), enlargement, *Holy Trinity*, Shirebrook, 1898-1904 .

Place, G.G., restoration, *St Peter*, Derby, 1851-3; restoration, *St Mary*, Chaddesden, 1858.

Platt, G., rebuild, *St Thomas á Becket*, Chapel-en-le-Frith, 1731-33.

Robinson, Frederick Josias (1833-1892) *see also Stevens & Robinson, below*, tower, *St Michael and All Angels*, Alsop-en-le-Dale, 1882-3; rebuilding, *St Bartholomew*, Hognaston, 1879-81; restoration, *St Helen*, Etwall, 1881; *St Giles*, Normanton-by-Derby, 1861?; *St Luke*, Derby,1872; rebuilding, *St Mary*, Newton Solney, 1880; enlargement, *Holy Trinity*, Middleton by Wirksworth.

Rollinson, Samuel, (1827-1891), north aisle and roof, *St Paul*, Hasland, 1866-67; chancel, *St Laurence*, Barlow, 1867; *Christ Church*, Chesterfield, 1869; *St Peter*, Calow, 1869; *St Michael and All Angels*, Sheldon, c1895.
& Sons, aisles *Christ Church*, Chesterfield, 1913-14; *St Mary*, Pilsley, 1873; nave and south aisle, *St Michael and All Angels*, South Normanton, 1878; rebuilding, *St James the Apostle*, Temple Normanton.

Rushforth, T.H., rebuild, *St Margaret of Antioch*, Wormhill, 1864.

Salvin, Anthony, (1827-1881), *All Saints*, Curbar, 1868; *St Katherine*, Rowsley, 1855.

Scott, George Gilbert,
George Gilbert Scott (1811-1878) was one of the great proponents of the Gothic revival in architecture. He is responsible for the Albert Memorial (1862-3), St Pancras Station (1865), the Martyrs Memorial in Oxford and the chapels of Exeter and St John's Colleges in Oxford. He also worked on the restoration of Ely, Chester, St David's, Gloucester, Lichfield, Rochester and Salisbury cathedrals. He was Professor of Architecture at the Royal Academy from 1866 to 1873.
Rebuilding, *St Peter*, Edensor, 1867; restoration, *St Mary and All Saints*, Chesterfield; north aisle, *St John the Baptist*, Staveley, 1865-9.

Scott, J. Oldrid, restoration, *St Mary the Virgin*, Denby, 1901-3.

Shaw, Norman, restoration, *St Giles*, Great Longstone, 1873, restoration, *All Saints*, Youlgreave, 1869-70; restoration, *St Alkmund*, Duffield, 1896; restoration, *St Werburgh*, 1891-2.

Sedding, J.D., restoration, *St John the Baptist*, Tideswell, early 1870s.

Shaw, Norman, restoration and bellcote, *Holy Cross*, Upper Langwith, 1877.

Shellard, H.E., *St Thomas*, Biggin, 1844-8; *St James*, 1844-6.

Smith, James (1830-41), rebuilding, *Holy Trinity*, Yeaveley.

St Aubyn, James Piers (1815-1895), restoration, *St Andrew*, Cubley, 1874; bellcote, *St Giles*, Marston Montgomery, 1875-7; restoration, *St Alkmund*, Duffield, 1846.

Stevens, H.I., *St James*, Shardlow & Great Wilne, 1838; *St John the Evangelist*, Hazelwood, 1840; *St George*, Ticknall, 1842; enlargement (with W. Evans), *St Michael and All Angels*, Shirley, 1842; repair, *St Chad*, Longford, 1843-44; *St Mary*, Coton-in-the-Elms, 1844-6; *Holy Trinity*, Clifton, 1845; *St Martin*, Osmaston, 1845; rebuilding and enlargement, *Christ Church*, Cotmanhay and Shipley, 1847-8; *Christ Church*, Belper, 1849; enlargement and north

aisle, *St Edmund*, Fenny Bentley, 1850; modernisation, *St Paul*, Little Eaton, 1851; *St Bartholomew*, Clay Cross, 1851; *All Saints*, Heath, 1853; enlargement and restoration, *St Helen*, Darley Dale, 1854; *St James*, Idridgehay, 1855; *St Michael and All Angels*, Alvaston, 1855-6; *St Michael and all Angels*, Alvaston, 1855-6; enlargement and north aisle, *St Peter*, Littleover, 1856 & 1908; design, *All Saints*, Mickleover, 1858-9; redesign, *St Mary*, Cromford, 1858.
& Robinson, F.J., *SS Philip and James*, Atlow, c1873; spire, *St Leonard*, Fenny Bentley, 1861; *All Saints*, Findern, 1863-64; *St Edmund*, Allestree, 1865-6; *St Lawrence*, Heanor, 1866-8; *St Peter*, Parwich, 1874; enlargement and north aisle, *St James*, Brassington, 1879-1885; rebuilding, *St Bartholomew*, Hognaston, 1879-81; north aisle, *Holy Trinity*, Tansley.

Streatfield, T.E., extension, *Holy Trinity*, Matlock Bath.

Street, G.E., enlargement, *St Laurence*, Long Eaton,1868; restoration, *All Saints*, Kirk Hallam, 1859; restoration *St Peter*, Derby, 1859; restoration, *St Mary*, Chaddesden, 1858.

Swinfin Barber, W., *St James*, New Mills, 1878-80.

Taylor, J.H. & H., rebuild, *Holy Trinity*, Ashford in the Water, 1868-70.

Taylor, M.H., *St Andrew*, Hadfield 1874.

Taylor (Isaac), Young (William Cecil) & Partners, restoration, *St Mary*, Bolsover 1961-2; repairs, *St Matthew*, Hayfield.

Townsend, C.C., *St Barnabas*, Bradwell, 1860s.

Turbutt, Gladwyn M.R., (d.1914), *St Chad*, Derby, 1881-2; enlargement, *Holy Cross*, Morton, 1912-1913.

Walker (Thomas Larkins, d.1860) & Goodacre (Robert Johnson, 1826-1904), *St Mary the Virgin*, Ilkeston, 1855.

Webster (John Dodsley, d.1913) & Son (Webster, John Douglas, b.1874), *St Mary*, Unstone, 1916-1921).

Weightman & Hadfield, *Holy Trinity*, Matlock Bath, 1842.

Whitaker, Glossop & Greaves, repairs to tower and spire, *Holy Trinity*, Edale, 1947-1948.

White, J., *St John the Baptist*, Buxton, 1811.

Widdows, Bernard, *St Luke*, Loscoe, 1936.

Wilson, Benjamin, *St Andrew*, Swanwick, 1860.

Woodhead, John (d. c1838)**& Hurst, William** (1787-1844), *St John the Evangelist*, Ridgeway, 1838-40; enlargement, *SS Peter and Paul*, Eckington.

Woods, Moses, *St Matthew*, Darley Abbey, 1818-9.

Woore, Peter, *St Nicholas*, Allestree, 1957-8.

Wyatt, T. H., *St Wystan*, Bretby, 1871.

Artists

Advent Hunstone
Late 19th and early 20th century. One of a family firm of woodcarvers in Tideswell and the best examples of his work are in the Tideswell church. He provided the woodwork and pews for a number of Derbyshire churches.

Bakewell, Robert, ironwork: *St Michael and all Angels*, Alvaston; *Derby Cathedral of All Saints*; *St Stephen*, Borrowash; communion rails, *St Saviour*, Foremark.

Burlison & Grylls, stained glass: *St Susanna*, Horsley Woodhouse; *St Mary the Virgin*, Ilkeston; *St Bartholomew*, Elvaston.

Burne-Jones, Edward, Coley, (1833-1898)
One of the leading designers and painters of his time and an important part of the 'Arts and Crafts' movement. Although he was considered one of the countries great painters in his own time, his most important influence today is probably through his contribution to ecclesiastical stained glass and furnishings. Much of the former was produced by Morris & Co to his designs.
Stained glass: *Holy Trinity*, Ashford in the Water; *All Saints*, Youlgreave; *All Saints*, Matlock Bank; *St Mary the Virgin*, Wirksworth.
Morris & Co, stained glass: *St Mary the Virgin*, South Darley; *St George*, Ticknall.

N. Comper, stained glass: *Holy Trinity*, Edale.

Davies, A.J., stained glass: *St Stephen*, Borrowash.

Gibbs, Charles, stained glass: *All Saints*, Mickleover.

Hemmings, A.O., painting and stained glass: *St Mary*, Cromford.

Jones & Willis, stained glass: *St Mary the Virgin*, Ilkeston.

Kempe, stained glass: *St Michael and All Angels*, Hathersage; *All Saints*, Youlgreave, *St James*, New Mills; *St Michael and All Angels*, Stanton by Dale.

Madox-Brown, Ford, stained glass: *Holy Trinity*, Tansley.

Nuttgens, J.E., stained glass: *SS Augustine*, Chesterfield; *St Anne*, Buxton; *St Cuthbert*, Doveridge; *St Thomas*, Derby.

Ramsey, W. stained glass: *St John*, Aldercar.

Tapper, Walter, woodwork: *St Mary*, Chaddesden; *St Peter*, Parwich; triptych, *St Mary*, Chaddesden.

Glossary

Advowson: The right to appoint the incumbent of a church. Often closely associated with *Impropriation* which is the right to receive income from *a benefice* – which can consist of one or more churches.

Apse: A semicircular, sometimes octagonal, end to a chancel.

Benefice: An ecclesiastical appointment that supplies an income to the holder.

Chancel: The eastern continuation of the nave. It contains the choir and altar and was traditionally reserved for the clergy.

Chantry: A chapel where masses are said for the soul(s) of a specific person or persons. Is often part of a larger church, in the form of a side chapel, but would usually have its own clergy.

Chapel of ease: A church built for the convenience of local inhabitants where the distance from the mother church is too great for easy access. The congregation would still be obliged to make financial contributions to the mother church and to attend there on the major festivals.

Decorated Gothic: An order of architecture prevalent from 1272 to 1377. Generally referred to simply as *Decorated*. It is characterised by the addition of pinnacles and parapets as well as ornate window tracery.

Early English: An order of architecture prevalent from 1145 to 1272. It is an early form of Gothic and is characterised by the appearance of pointed arches, clusters of pillars and lancet windows set in groups of three, five or seven.

Ecclesia: The preReformation term for a parish church or *rectory* (see below).

Ecclesiastical parish: The oldest form of organised local government in this country, though in more recent times the secular aspects of this have been taken over by the Civil parish and the Ecclesiastical parish is simply that area for which a local church has spiritual responsibility.

Gothic: The architecture that prevailed between 1200 and 1500. This is usually subdivided into styles into three periods: *Early English*, *Decorated* and *Perpendicular*. The Gothic Revival of the 19th century, was a movement to revive these forms of architecture. Architects either attempted to follow one of the three orders above or borrowed elements such as pointed arches, gargoyles, steeply pitched roves and elaborate brickwork to create a style known as *Victorian Gothic*.

Narthex: An entry area or vestibule at the east end of a church.

Nave: The main body of a church.

Norman: An order of architecture introduced from the continent at the time of the Norman invasion. It was heavily influenced by Roman architecture with an emphasis on heavy rounded arches and prevailed from 1066 to 1145.

Saxon: The church architecture which prevailed in this country prior to the Norman invasion. Covers the period approximately 800 – 1066.

Perpendicular Gothic: An order of architecture prevalent from 1350 to 1539. This is the most elaborate form of Gothic, characterised by large windows with elaborate tracery, high arches and wide interiors with parapets and flying buttresses outside. Usually referred to simply as *Perpendicular*.

Rectory: The original term generally referred to combined rights of *Advowson* and *Impropriation*. The holder of these rights, the rector, could appoint a deputy, a vicar, to carry out the duty of ministering to the church itself, and allocate a portion of the benefice income to him. This portion would be a *vicarage*, see below.

Retro-choir: The area in a cathedral behind the choir.

Transepts: In a cruciform church, these refer to the 'arms' pointing north and south.

Tympanum: A semicircular area above a doorway, often containing carvings or sculpture. With carvings, it is especially typical of Norman churches.

Vicarage: Originally a smaller benefice, within a *rectory*, that supplied an income to the rector's deputy, the vicar. A church whose income was used to support a vicar would be referred to as a *vicarage*. Now of course, the term refers to the house in which a vicar lives.